CLINTON

LA
LA

MY FAMILY, A SYMPHONY

A MEMOIR OF GLOBAL ADOPTION

AARON ESKE

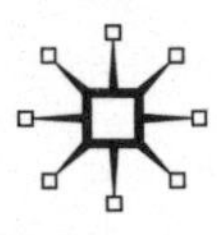

MY FAMILY, A SYMPHONY

First published in 2010 by PALGRAVE MACMILLAN® in the U.S.—a division of St. Martin's Press LLC, 175 Fifth Avenue, New York, NY 10010.

Where this book is distributed in the UK, Europe and the rest of the world, this is by Palgrave Macmillan, a division of Macmillan Publishers Limited, registered in England, company number 785998, of Houndmills, Basingstoke, Hampshire RG21 6XS.

Palgrave Macmillan is the global academic imprint of the above companies and has companies and representatives throughout the world.

ISBN 978-0-230-10415-0

Library of Congress Cataloging-in-Publication Data is available from the Library of Congress.

A catalogue record of the book is available from the British Library.

Design by Letra Libre

First edition: December 2010

10 9 8 7 6 5 4 3 2 1

Printed in the United States of America.

To the Memory of

Lenore Anita Kyle Thomas

In Whose Beautiful and Delicate Life

There Is the Perfection

That Endures

CONTENTS

PROLOGUE

We the people love a good orphan story. So much so that as I write this, twenty-five of the fifty all-time highest-grossing movies where I live in the United States feature an orphaned protagonist. We're captivated by parentless tales of the Caped Crusader, a hobbit from the shire, a Jedi Knight from a galaxy far, far away, and the boy with a scar on his forehead who lived to defeat He-Who-Must-Not-Be-Named. Ever since baby Moses drifted along the banks of the Nile and into the Pharaoh's palace, countless fantastical orphans have grown so intertwined in our collective heritage that we know their stories by heart.

Once upon a time . . . Cinderella lived with two ugly stepsisters, broke curfew, and married a prince. Tom Sawyer lived with his Aunt Polly, pretended to pirate the Mississippi River, and befriended the half-orphan Huck Finn. Annie sang about her hard-knock life, wore a red wig, and moved in with the bald Daddy Warbucks. And orphan Dorothy went over the rainbow, stole some fabulous shoes, and immortalized the saying, "There's no place like home."

In some stories the reader feels compelled to pick up a pitiful orphan like Oliver from the sooty page and give him a home and a good meal. And in other popular fables like King Arthur and

Spiderman, it's the orphan who rescues us. Without their parents, these superheroes are the world's orphans and, as they see it, the world's avengers. Superman is the steel model for this mold, but his story stands out from the literary orphan tradition for reasons other than his red cape and kryptonite allergy. In the realm of orphan fantasy, Clark Kent is the rare international adoptee, interplanetary even, who as payback for the chance to grow up with loving parents, assumes the values of his adopted homeland in his never-ending battle for truth, justice, and the American way.

I HAVE MY OWN STORY ABOUT ORPHANS that is a little different from all of the others. Although my quest involves some villains and each hero in my story has a weakness, my narrative isn't like Batman's or Frodo's or Harry Potter's. That's because the orphans in my life are nonfictional. They are my brother and sisters, and this is our family's memoir.

It might embarrass my family members and me, but all the facts and memories in this story are true and, of course, as in most memoirs, the point of view is my own. As for the incidents that may seem too absurd to be true, they have been verified and are every bit as accurate as the rest. I learned from an early age to believe in unbelievable realities. Like when my brother was kidnapped as a baby because of his light skin tone, and my sister was robbed while hitching a ride on top of a train going 70 miles per hour through an Indian jungle, and my other sister was supposed to have a surgical pirate peg leg installed after she was born to a runaway dwarf but instead grew up halfway around the world to become a dancer with her own two feet. I know it might sound a little crazy at this moment, but read on and I promise it will all come together, just as my family has, like a symphony with many movements that sometimes go in different directions but were all composed to be one in the end.

~

Before I end this preamble, I have one last note. Because this story is partly theirs, 25 percent of the author's royalties of this book are being donated to all the orphaned children in Holt International's care. I will forever be in awe of and debt to this organization that does so much to give kids worldwide a family. So now you can feel even better about buying a copy for all of your friends if you like it—which I'm sure you will because, if you're anything like the rest of us, you love a good orphan story, even if you didn't know that until now.

Chapter One

ALBUM K

LENORE WORE A TIARA TO HER EIGHTIETH birthday party. It crowned her angelic white hair. The wife of a gregarious minister and the mother of two, she played the role of the lovely wallflower at most of life's celebrations, but this day was her blooming day. If her husband, my grandfather, had been there, he would have said something about what it was like to grow shorter together, but Alzheimer's stole his voice, mind, and life before they had the chance to find out. Now it was her turn to do the talking to the full room of relatives, former bridesmaids, and her new eighty-eight-year-old boyfriend.

"I'm a lucky lady," she said. "Terrific family, terrific friends, a new hip." She popped it sideways to show it off. "I have a beautiful life."

Whenever I went to my grandmother's house at Eastmont Towers Retirement Community in Lincoln, I looked at that beautiful life, neatly chronicled in fourteen photo albums labeled "A" to "N" and displayed within easy reach on her bookshelf. The sticky pages traced her black-and-white beginnings in Great Depression Omaha, her two-year stint on an air force base in reconstruction Korea, and onward to the Boeing homecomings of her colorful grandchildren from three Asian countries.

Grandmother Lenore's albums told the story of the century. And as interesting as Albums "A" to "J" of the 1900s were, Album "K" was still my biased favorite. Bound in furry brown velvet, K's pages were the storyboard of my life growing up with four adopted siblings. We were best friends then—before I fled them and lost touch.

You could guess the year each photo in Album K was taken by which house was in the background. With every new child in my family came a new house with another bedroom until at last all five of us were home. The album's first picture was dated 1983, but the clues in the photograph said more than the caption ever could. Mom's blond hair was crimped and long like Bon Jovi's without the bangs. A black Groucho Marx moustache sat on Dad's less stiff upper lip. They were holding me, their first and only biological child, whom they'd made the old-fashioned way.

I was an only child when we lived on B Street in a tannish fixer-upper in Lincoln, Nebraska—a quaint city in the heart of the Heartland. At the time, a street map of Lincoln showed a tall rectangular grid much like that of Manhattan, but that was about the only thing the two places had in common. From the top of the three tallest buildings in the city, you didn't have to squint to see the flat and forever prairie in the near distance stretching beyond the city limits. The good people of Lincoln would say they were just that—"real good people"—who worked hard but not too hard, enjoyed a medium-well-done steak a few times a week, and aimed to live life simple and right. Weekends were for worship—Sunday to Jesus and Saturday to the Cornhusker football team. Meanwhile, I liked spending my weekend mornings eating Coco-Puffs and watching Rainbow Brite and the Smurfs light up our 13-channel TV set.

Around the time I slung my Bert and Ernie backpack over my shoulder for my first day of school, Mom and Dad had the urge to have another child, and they didn't care where that child came from—as long as it wasn't from Mom's uterus. Pregnancy and childbirth were on Mom's list of never-doing-that-agains right below riding a motorcycle and living in Texas. They all resulted in too much pain. When their application for adoption was approved, my parents told me I would be getting a new sister, but the news didn't faze me. They might as well have said, "Aaron, we ordered a V-neck sweater from the Lands' End catalog and it should arrive in the next few weeks." I was too young to understand what it meant to add a family member, let alone care which country's seal was stamped on her passport cover.

The day after my family moved to our next house, on Marilynn Avenue, my parents painted the walls an avant-garde navy in contrast to the Motel 6ish floral wallpaper that draped our neighbors' bedrooms. A few weeks after the paint dried, the metal United Airlines stork delivered us Meredith Leslie—a nine-month-old girl from India named after her two grandfathers. I was six.

When Meredith arrived on our doorstep, her left leg looked like a gnawed turkey drumstick you might eat at the state fair, and two of her fingertips were attached to each other, as if by superglue. The birthmarks were nothing that half the doctors in Nebraska couldn't try to fix, though.

Hooked on adoption, my parents called the adoption agency a year later, and our family brought home two older children from India, Michelle and Jordan. They were biological siblings with invented birthdays and trauma beyond their unknown years. Crowded again, we all migrated to the southern tip of town into a Pepto-Bismol-pink house on Elk Ridge Road. Every other house on the street was taupe, but Mom and Dad didn't mind. It may have been a Barbie mansion, but it had five bedrooms and a laundry room on the same level. Dad practiced law full-time, and when Mom wasn't at work directing the state's Department of Health and Human Services, she was at home directing ours. They needed every shortcut they could get to manage four children under the age of ten. Being able to load towels in the dryer and shout out bedtime stories at the same time was a priceless amenity.

For the first few years in the pink house, a sweet family of heifers and their trusty steer we called "Butch and the Babes" grazed behind our backyard in an open field. But Lincoln's grid was growing and cows weren't part of the development plan. About the time the bulldozers rolled onto Butch's turf and unearthed four decades of manure that smelled so strong you could taste the shit on your spit, we added baby Jamie to our herd. She was a fourteen-month-old Korean girl named after her father, James. Since our lodging was over capacity again and life smelled like a stockyard, we moved to Water Tower Court (the street had its own water tower) just outside Lincoln, where cornstalks twice my height grew adjacent to our new homestead.

The 6,000-square-foot home (1,000 for each of us kids) with its Taj Mahal architecture and Romeo and Juliet balconies was as dramatic as the memories it would house. At Water Tower, what had been a family sitcom swerved toward soap opera, and we lost our way. For reasons no one could comprehend at the time, Michelle was the first to flare up. Then Jordan. Then Meredith. No matter how much love and energy she poured over the flames, Mom couldn't contain my family's destruction. And I couldn't understand the causes and didn't want to try. As soon as I escaped the state, and Michelle ran away from home, and Jordan was shipped off to the army, and Meredith started then stopped college, Mom put down the hose, surrendered, and retreated. My parents phoned

Chet's Movers, enrolled Jamie in a new middle school, and began life anew in a cookie-cutter house with three bedrooms and an unlisted phone number on a gated street an hour away from my new hometown of Omaha.

The final photo in Album K was taken at the house on Water Tower. It was Christmas Day 2004, the last time I could remember us five in the same room together. In the Christmas picture's background, you could see the polytheistic shrine of the Water Tower house hovering behind our heads. There was Pope John Paul II's framed autograph, a candleless menorah, and a white marble statuette of the Hindu Sai Baba. Clearly Mom and Dad embraced multiculturalism in every area of life—even home decor. Secular Christianity was the clear winner of the day though, as the five of us "kids," whose ages ranged from ten to twenty-one, gathered beside the star-topped, present-bottomed tree like most families in America.

In the picture, I am wearing my collegiate black-frame glasses. I was five months away from graduating from the University of Nebraska. My snowy December skin looks pale and flavorless compared to my siblings' Hershey-brown tones. A seventeen-year-old Jordan stands to my right. His smile is pursed, naughtily. The girls, all with faces prime for *Vogue* but not the long legs for runway, hunch low in front. Looking at our pose you might wonder what perverted reality TV producer had brought these five adolescents together on Christmas morning. But when I looked back at us, because it was another normally abnormal scene in my life, I just wondered which one of us got the best presents that year.

After I graduated from the University of Nebraska, I moved to Washington, D.C., for work and then to London for school, putting more and more miles between my family and myself. I never consciously chose to move farther away. Honestly, I never even considered the distance. It didn't matter to me at the time. I was fine on my own.

Flash forward to Omaha 2008, a different era, when a black man was running for president of the United States of America, China was hosting the Olympics, and my siblings and I were all together again for our grandmother, who was hoisting a glass of chardonnay above her head on her birthday. "So thank you for traveling across the country, well around the world actually," grandmother Lenore and I locked eyes, "to be here with me today."

WHEN I FLEW BACK FOR MY grandmother's birthday party, I didn't just fly to Nebraska in eight hours direct from England. For one thing, that wouldn't make much of a story. But I also couldn't have found my way home that way, not the way I wanted to. Instead, I bought a round-the-world ticket to trace the orphan origins of my family.

I didn't speak to any of my siblings before I boarded that first airplane bound for their home countries. I never called my sister to say, "I'm about to meet the woman who changed your diapers." I had fallen out of touch with all four of them, and I wanted back in.

The party room at the French Café in Omaha's gentrified slaughterhouse district gargled up an off-key "Happy Birthday" chorus, and I heard someone whistle and guessed it was my sister Michelle. Public outings were always spectacles in our family—which was why we reserved our own space in the back. Thankfully, the rest of the restaurant was also empty. Apparently not many people in Nebraska go for French food at five o'clock on a Saturday. There was probably a football game on.

The party mingling recommenced, and my siblings and I slinked into a corner of the brick-walled room and huddled beneath a life-size portrait of a nude woman sitting on a pile of white pillows. A soft pink flower was shoved behind her painted ear. The air conditioning blasted to combat the August heat.

A second cousin came around to take our picture, and we posed just as we had the last time we were all together, on that Christmas morning four years before. This time though, my cheeks, neck, ribs, and wrists were gaunt from circumnavigating the globe. I had lost twenty-five pounds on the journey and weight-wise was only five-sixths of the already small person I had been before. To my right was Jordan, twenty-one, whose biceps (unlike mine) had grown in proportion to his years. The army did a body good. His teeth shone. My sisters posed down in front, still stunning but just as genetically gifted in a game of limbo as they had always been. They wore the beaded necklaces I'd bought for them from a jewelry *patua* I'd met in monsoon Mumbai the month before.

Once the amateur photo shoot ended and it was just us again, I opened my bag and pulled out the used tea box wrapped in packing tape.

"I know it's not your eightieth birthday, but this is for you guys. From Mrs. Joshi."

"What is it?"

"No idea. I've carried it around the world and all I know is it's heavy."

Michelle took the box and looked up at me. "So why are you doing this anyway? Why go to India and Korea and Japan and China and Ethi-, Ethiapulous?"

"Ethiopia?"

"Yeah, why go all those places?"

Before boarding my flight from London to Delhi and launching a twenty-three-city world tour, I wouldn't have been sure how to answer her. Had I actually picked up the phone and had a conversation with my sister at the time, the best response I could have given her would have sounded something like, "I guess I'm bored" or "I'm sick of ordering take-out Chinese and want to taste the real thing." But of course there was something deeper that drove me to fly 24,901 miles. I had to rediscover what connected us all those years ago. I remembered the details of being each other's best friends. In the morning we'd rinse our tiny toothbrushes under the same faucet and after school we'd all walk home single file through the sewage tunnels that snaked through our neighborhood. But because of what had happened to us, the memories no longer felt real. They were nothing more than a 4 × 6 glossy stuck in an album named "K." Mere artifacts like the contents of the moving boxes stored in our parents' new basement. I was twenty-four and my relationship with my family was already collecting dust.

To know what . . . no, to *feel* what I was missing, I couldn't simply return to Nebraska. You may think it's inside-out that to get closer to my family I traveled even farther away. Now that I have written the words down, it looks more foolish than ever. But I knew in my heart that I had to start my journey where theirs had begun twenty years earlier and come full circle. To regain the family I once had with the four most influential people in my life, I needed to figure out our separate and common past.

Chapter Two

FOOTSTEPS

THE FIRST ORPHAN TRAIN, BOUND FOR DOWAGIAC, Michigan, carried forty-six orphans, waifs, and street urchins who had scarcely seen an open field in their lives when the locomotive pulled out of the New York City train depot in 1854. Its ten- to twelve-year-old passengers came from the city's children's asylums, newsboys' lodging houses, jails, and downtown doorways. At the time, 30,000 abandoned and orphaned children slept in these living tombs, temporarily at least. Half of them died before their fifth birthday. The contaminated and teeming city was drowning in the tide of immigration, and there was simply too little for too many. Then came the orphan trains and the start of the first humanitarian migration of children to be cared for by their adoptive families in the United States.

But before exploring what it was like in the 1800s for orphans to relocate to states across America such as Nebraska, allow me to introduce you to a young brown-bearded seminary graduate from the class of 1849. Charles Loring Brace at first hoped to reform the ills of New York City through the ministry, but he found his true calling away from the pulpit, in the extreme squalor of the city's streets. After working in the dense shade of disease, prostitution, and murder in Manhattan's Five Points slum, Brace realized that his real mission was not to cleanse the sin but to evacuate the innocent so they might be spared.

One of those innocents was Ann "Mabel" Harrison, who, at the time I met her, was ninety-nine years old. She lived in my eighty-year-old grandmother Lenore's retirement community in Lincoln—ninety-seven years after she rode an orphan train across Nebraska to Colorado to a new life. The skin around her eye sockets was a clean pink and her face was nearly lineless except for a comb-like row of wrinkles on her upper lip that disappeared when she smiled. When recalling a high-heeled 1936 walk down New York City's Lexington Avenue, she touched her temple with her manicured fingertips, charging her memory. Mabel, a redhead who went by her confirmation name of Ann, had been pursuing an opera career in the city in 1936.

"I was simply walking down Lexington Avenue there," she said, "and looked up and saw it was St. Vincent Ferrer Church and I remember that my father once said that's where I was baptized." She never wondered why a girl from Colorado Springs, Colorado, would be baptized in New York, New York, because, "Well, I was brought up to never ask questions."

At age twenty-seven, she entered the church to start asking questions. When the priest returned from looking for Ann's baptismal certificate, he told her, "We have no record of you," and directed her to the New York Foundling Hospital two blocks away.

"Oh yes, you were here," the sister at the Foundling Hospital said. Ann Harrison was born Mabel Cohen to an unmarried Jennie Rubin, a nineteen-year-old Russian immigrant, and Moe Cohen, twenty-one, of 604 Eastern Parkway in Brooklyn. They delivered her into the care of the New York Foundling Hospital when she was nine days old; she was one of ten children handed over that day. Her adoptive parents managed to keep the adoption a secret, as was common then. It would have been difficult to conceal Ann's adoption from her had they stayed in Colorado very long. But Ann's mother was battling tuberculosis, and the family kept migrating south to warmer and drier climates to subdue the symptoms. The disease consumed her mother when Ann was eleven. Her adoptive father would die two years after Ann discovered the truth about her adopted life. She never spoke to him about her walk down Lexington Avenue, however. She didn't feel she needed to.

"Afterwards, I looked at my reflection in a window of a store and said, 'Hmm, don't look any different,' and sort of just laughed about it." She laughed about it again, seventy-two years later, and the comb-ish row of wrinkles stretched into absence. At her last count, Ann personally knew of two other surviving orphan train riders—the historical ancestors of today's international adoptees in America.

Charles Loring Brace's actions, which gave New York's struggling street children a new chance at survival, personified a theory that Charles Darwin was brewing at the exact same time an ocean away. In his *On the Origin of Species,* published in 1859, Darwin wrote,

> Owing to this struggle for life, any variation, however slight and from whatever cause proceeding, if it be in any degree profitable to an individual of any species, in its infinitely complex relations to other organic beings and to external nature, will tend to the preservation of that individual, and will generally be inherited by its offspring. The offspring, also, will thus have a better chance of surviving, for, of the many individuals of any species which are periodically born, but a small number can survive. I have called this principle, by which each slight variation, if useful, is preserved, by the term of Natural Selection, in order to mark its relation to man's power of selection.[1]

By the time Brace's last orphan train arrived at its final destination seventy-five years later, 200,000 New York City children like Ann Mabel Harrison had been preserved by a man-made variation of natural selection. They'd all been transplanted to the homes of Christian farm families in forty-seven states, their futures no longer bound by their origins.

Some children were assigned a family before they boarded the trains, but many only knew which city was printed on their train ticket. The orphan riders with assigned families had their names, birthdays, and new home addresses sewn into the linings of their coats or the hems of their dresses. On June 19, 1911, at 1:00 PM, John Joseph Gruele and Anna Waters Gruele waited at the train station to receive their red-headed daughter with a patch sewn on her dress that said, "Mabel," just as my parents waited at the airport in 1989, 1991, and 1996 to meet their children for the first time.

MORE THAN A CENTURY before Charles Darwin theorized how species are selected for survival, another Englishman was setting an example that started the evolution of humanitarianism. His name was Thomas Coram, and he was the founder of the world's first incorporated charity, the Foundling Hospital in London. His historic work would affect many orphans' lives, as well as my own.

When I moved to London, I lived first in an international residence hall with a plaque out front that tickled tourists. They would point to the dormitory sign—Goodenough College—and pose for pictures while wearing the Penn State sweatshirts they'd been given for graduation or the Oxford University sweatshirts they'd bought from a souvenir stall at Oxford Circus that morning. By British standards, the name could have been worse. After all, this is a country with centuries-old streets with names like Butt Hole Road.

Located in Dickensian Bloomsbury south of King's Cross Station, the place looked like a palace. It had brick towers, balconies, and its own grassy garden. Living there was like living in any ordinary residence, well . . . almost. I'm not sure how ordinary it was to wake up to the Polish guy in #239 practicing for his harpsichord recital while a nasal buffet of breakfast pho and porridge crawled up the plumbing from the community kitchen downstairs.

My room overlooked Coram's Fields, a large square park enclosed by a six-story wall of oak trees with leaves that rustled me to sleep when Huang next door called home every night to tell China good morning. I called home to Nebraska once a week. When I did, I would get updates from my parents about Meredith beginning beauty school or Jordan dating a stripper who worked at the bar in Louisiana where he guarded the door as a bouncer.

"You should talk to them more," they'd say. "They're your siblings. They want to be a part of your life."

"Yeah," I'd agree.

A psychoanalyst might deduce that I had moved to London to wedge the Atlantic Ocean between my new life and my past, but she'd be wrong. In truth, I had a scholarship to study abroad and I liked the accent. Besides, I didn't need six time zones to feel distant from my siblings—we had stopped talking years ago even when we still lived in the same state. They sometimes tried contacting me, but I rarely tried in return. On my birthday my sister Michelle wrote me, "Hope you had a fabilious birthday and hope you're having a great time in England. Miss you much Big brother." I never replied.

I was comfortable on my own in my Goodenough room overlooking the rustling leaves. After I'd lived there for a few months, the fifty-foot curtain of leaves began to fall and for the first time I could glimpse the full insides of the park outside the window. Attached to the park's gated entrance was another sign popular with tourists that read, "Coram's Fields: No Unaccompanied Adults." *Adults* was underlined in red. A guard minded the gate and kept watch over the park's very important little persons.

Unless I was with a child, I couldn't enter the park, so my image of it was framed by what I could see from my window in wintertime. Through the naked tree branches, I could see a shallow reflecting pool lining the center and leading to a mint-roofed gazebo. On a few occasions I witnessed by sight and smell a pair of black sheep roaming the grounds, aloof from the metropolis in their midst. I also could have sworn I heard a peacock squawk once, but it might have been a pigeon having a bad day.

Curious to know more than my senses could tell me about this forbidden park, I did what any savvy grad student would do and searched for "Coram's Fields" on Wikipedia. "Situated on the former site of the Foundling Hospital, established by Thomas Coram in what was then named Lamb's Conduit Fields in 1739," the web page said. Later that night in bed, as I tried to block out the sound of Huang laughing with his sister on speakerphone, I couldn't shake the questions that kept leaping in my mind. *What was so special about this Foundling Hospital? Are these foundlings like orphans? Who was Thomas Coram and why is there a park named in his honor that won't allow me inside?* I reopened my laptop to learn more.

In Thomas Coram's portrait, he looked like a grandfather, although he had no children. White feathery hair dusted his shoulders and framed his friendly face and the round brown eyes that gazed out to the ships in the distance. A bronze medallion engraved with the image of the pharaoh's daughter and her maids coming upon baby Moses in the bulrushes dangled from Coram's right hand.

I learned that the Foundling Hospital had received its first child at 8:00 PM on March 25, 1741. The opening of the hospital was the close of a nineteen-year-old daydream that started when Coram was walking home to his wife, Eunice, through the cobblestone streets of East London in 1722. The stench of a thousand wet horses would have masked the smell of human sewage that trickled in the gutters on its way to the Thames. Tightly packed tenement housing aligned the winding alleyways. The buildings had been erected in a hurry after the Great Fire of 1666 destroyed most of the city, and they were supposed to be temporary. Yet the ones that hadn't collapsed and buried their sleeping tenants were still in use sixty years later, serving as the architectural ancestors of the world's city slums today.

On that night in 1722, Coram saw an infant lying in the sludge nearby. The newborn's mother had likely left the child in the street, hoping someone with more means would take pity on her foundling. But the time for pity had expired and the baby was now just one more corpse polluting Little Trinity Lane. At the time, only one in four children born in London lived beyond their fifth birthday. Unable to look at the lifeless figure, Coram stared up above the rows and rows of hovels and saw the dome of St. Paul's Cathedral shimmering in the lamplight.

For the next two decades, Coram pitched his vision of constructing a hospital for foundlings to London's elite. Most West Enders, in their wide hoop skirts and red-painted noble heels, would never fathom walking around the city's cruel shipping wharfs the way Coram did. They knew little and cared less about the subclass of children of which Thomas Coram spoke. Over time, however, Coram did attract a few aristocratic sympathizers to his cause, and with their signatures and financial support he petitioned King George II for permission to erect "houses and hospitals for maintaining and educating bastard children." The king granted the request in 1739, making the sixty-nine-year-old Thomas Coram the founder of the world's first-ever incorporated charity. Two years later, he had his home for children on fifty-six acres of pasture on the northern edge of London.

The suspended doorbell to the Foundling Hospital rang shortly after eight o'clock on the night of March 25, 1741. A mother encased in a black silk hood lovingly abandoned her infant in a cubbyhole and disappeared into the crowd that had congregated to watch the historic event. Twenty-nine mothers followed her lead, and by midnight the hospital was at capacity. When the Foundling Hospital received the last infant of the night, the random spectators sauntered back toward the sound and smoke of the city. A few women lingered, dejected, in the field among the sleeping sheep. They cradled their ungiven babies.

FOR ALMOST TWO CENTURIES MORE, tens of thousands of foundlings passed by the portrait of Coram wearing his rusty red waistcoat as they were carried through the hospital's reception chamber during their first few days on Earth. In 1925, uncomfortably surrounded by London's growth, the Foundling Hospital relocated, to the city's countryside once more. In its hallowed place, the city opened a park reserved explicitly for children, where no unattended adults were allowed, and a residence hall for international students.

How bizarre, I thought, and closed my laptop before climbing back into bed in that very residence hall for international students that sat atop the fossils of the world's first government-formalized orphanage. While I shifted in the sheets to find a comfortable position lying on the springy mattress that had probably been used by one of Goodenough's first residents decades ago, I listened to Huang, who was still laughing on the phone with his family in the room next door. I wondered what my siblings, my own modern-day orphans, were doing in Nebraska at this precise moment. *I'll call them tomorrow,* I told myself and then got back to trying to fall asleep.

I couldn't remember if we had a bon voyage family dinner the night before I moved out of Nebraska in 2005. Couldn't remember piling my bed or books or the handmade blue blanket Michelle had given me into the seventeen-foot U-Haul. Couldn't remember which family members were standing there on the Water Tower driveway to wave me goodbye as I put the giant truck in reverse. If it weren't for the pictures I took with my camera phone on my way to Washington, D.C., I wouldn't even have remembered the drive through the wild fields of purple thistle in Iowa or the fuzzy green Appalachian Mountains in Pennsylvania. The memories did not start again until I was in my new apartment making my bed. I remembered folding Michelle's blanket in two and laying it at the foot of the bed atop a white comforter. I sat on it and poked my fingers through the holes in the crocheted threads. I didn't feel homesick. Just felt like I should.

When I woke up the next morning in Goodenough College, I picked up my phone, which was charging on the floor beside my bed. I sat on the bed's edge poking my fingers through the holes in Michelle's blanket as I dialed with my free hand. Now I did feel homesick. For years I had avoided the struggle of relating to my family and understanding why. . . . Why going home for family birthday parties and spending time close together pushed me farther away from them. Why I no longer felt like I belonged in my family at all. But at Goodenough, surrounded by my global neighbors and the history of orphan care across the street, it became impossible to avoid the whys, and I had no choice but to confront my questions and learn to re-relate.

"Hi, I'd like to fly around the world," I told the travel agent on the phone. "Can you help me?"

EVERY HUNDRED YEARS OR SO, somewhere in the world an ordinary person seems to have the inspiration to advance the evolution of adoption. Thomas Coram crossed social strata to build the first home for foundlings in mid-eighteenth-century London. Charles Loring Brace's orphan trains crossed the country in mid-nineteenth-century America. And more recently, Bertha and Harry Holt crossed an ocean in the mid-twentieth century to share their home in Oregon with a brood of orphaned children from Korea. Somehow, the legacies of each of these revolutionaries have crossed my life.

Grandma Holt, as everyone called her, stayed the weekend with my family in 1993. She was eighty-nine. I was ten. After she finished her jog around our neighborhood, Bertha asked Mom to take her to the hair salon. "I need a new 'do," she said.

"Sure," Mom said. "What kind?"

"Same as always. High up top. Braids on the sides."

An hour later Bertha was back from the salon with a perfect Heidi beehive. The same style she had sported forty years earlier while making a decision that ever since has affected the lives of millions of people.

As she wrote in her detailed autobiography *The Seed from the East,* Bertha paced the thirteen rooms of the Oregon farmhouse her husband had built. It was April. She imagined a cot in the library corner, an extra table in the dining room. She already had six biological children, many still living at home, but she wanted more. Not only that—she believed her Lord wanted her to have more. Her husband, Harry, who *Time* magazine would later describe as "a thickset man with a ragged mustache and shaggy eyebrows," approached her and looked out the tall window at the spring wheat fields, still yellow and bristly.

"I think we ought to adopt some of the G.I. children," he said.

"That's the way I feel, too."

The way Bertha recalled the conversation in her autobiography, Harry then asked, "How many do you think we could take care of?"

Bertha pondered her petite hands, weathered by fifty-one years of life on the farm. She had been born in Des Moines, Iowa, at the dawn of the twentieth century and married her cousin Harry Holt of Neligh, Nebraska, on New Year's Eve, two years before the stock market crash. Their first family home was a cook shack on wheels in South Dakota, a state on the outer rim of the dust bowl and a northern notch on the Midwestern Bible Belt. The storms of depression and dust became too much, and Bertha and Harry bought land in Oregon, where they raised their six children.

The cause of Bertha's unrest that spring morning in her Oregon farmhouse was a lecture she and Harry had recently attended. It was presented by Dr. Bob Pierce, who a few years prior had founded the religious humanitarian organization World Vision. Dr. Pierce was back from Korea and spoke in the Holt children's high school auditorium about the plight of Amer-Asian babies in the freshly postwar country. The children's fathers were American GIs who were fighting in the Korean War. When the war ended and the men returned home, they left behind Korean mothers with babies who did not fit into the country's society. To be a mixed-race child in the United States in 1955 was taboo. In Korea, it was a death sentence. After the lecture, when they tried to fall asleep, neither Bertha nor Harry could forget the image of a child nearly hidden beneath a pile of garbage. Flies swarmed the infant's dirty pale skin. His mother had thrown him away because his eyes were blue. There were countless other children in Korea like him.

At last Bertha spoke and bid low. "I suppose we could care for six of the Korean war orphans."

"Oh my, we have plenty of room for eight, or ten, or even more," Harry said.

All the blonde hairs on her head would have stood up had they not been tied down in her usual Heidi braid.

Harry and Bertha concluded they could care for eight babies from Korea, and they wrote to Washington to start the adoption process. Welfare agency officials came out to the farm to explain that, legally, the Holts could adopt only two children from overseas. And even that was going to be tricky. Between 1935 and 1948, fewer than 200 total immigrants entered the United States in the category "under 16 years of age, unaccompanied by parents." It is unknown how many of these were international children adopted by American families. Even if they all were, the low number still shows the extreme rarity of international adoption. Following World War II, the United States passed the Displaced Persons Act of 1948 to allow 200,000 European refugees and 3,000 displaced orphans to enter the country. Five years later, entangled in another war (this time in Korea), Congress passed the Refugee Relief Act, which granted 4,000 orphan visas. Hopeful parents were only allowed to adopt two children from Korea. But that didn't suit the Holts' dream.

To adopt their eight children, the Holts were told they would have to ask both houses of Congress to change the law. "Then that's what we'll do," Bertha said and wrote to Washington once more.

Oregon Senator Richard Neuberger replied in June 1955,

> I regret that the process of adopting special legislation in the Congress is time-consuming and presents a distressing delay. Such legislation must be considered by the Senate Judiciary Committee, Senate Immigration Committee, and the Senate, itself, and then it repeats a similar process in the House of Representatives before being signed by the President. I know of no other way to proceed, than that which I have outlined above.

Congress was going to adjourn in July—giving Bertha one more month to pass all the improbably high bars. The challenge didn't dissuade her motherly determination, for she already felt these were to be her children. So she would do all she could. Plus, her husband was already in Korea searching for them.

Harry had received his passport, sponsored missionary visa, and vaccinations; he refused to waste a day that could save his child's life while waiting for welfare's bureaucracy. So he flew to Seoul to begin his search for his eight children—four boys and four girls. He didn't know who the children were, but he believed his God would give him the strength and time to find them. After all, judging by his medical record of repeated heart attacks, he shouldn't even have been alive. For years, doctors had warned him against "rigorous" activities like walking in the sand, so a journey to Korea would push him to the max. But Harry viewed his quest as the reason God was keeping him alive. Rescuing these children was his purpose on the planet.

A letter from Harry:

June 1955

To my dear ones: We landed at Tokyo about 9:30. Everything went fine. . . .

At 3:30 yesterday afternoon I had my first opportunity to lie down for a little rest. The next thing I knew it was 9 o'clock. I just stayed in bed without supper. I awakened about three this morning but that was all right as I had much to think about. . . .

The enemy was giving me a good working over. He seemed to say, "What are you doing out here away from home? You are nothing but a farmer and not a very good one at that. . . ."

As these thoughts filled my mind I became very discouraged and I finally slipped out of bed and knelt down and poured my distress out to the Lord. That didn't seem to help very much and I finally said, 'Lord, my faith is very small this morning. Will You show me from Your Word whether I'm doing this myself or whether You are with me?' Then I shook my Bible open and put my thumb on part of the page and turned on the light. . . .

'Fear not for I am with thee. . . . I will bring thy seed from the east, and gather thee from the west; I will say to the north, Give up; and to the south, Keep not back: bring my sons from afar, and my daughters from the ends of the earth; Even every one that is called by my name: for I have created him for my glory, I have formed him; yea, I have made him. . . . '

I just had to get down and weep before the Lord. Love, Daddy.

Soon after she received her husband's letter, Bertha set down the red onion she was peeling to answer the phone.

"Mrs. Holt," said the reporter from the *Eugene Register Guard*, "We have a telegram from Senator Neuberger, which says that he and Senator Morse introduced special legislation in the Senate yesterday to allow your husband and you to adopt and bring to the United States eight Korean War orphans."

She had cleared the first bar. There was a bill.

"We'd like to send a photographer," the man on the phone continued.

"Oh, we're not nice looking," she said. "And I'm only a farmer's wife. But the children will be home from haying around five."

June 12, 1955

I wish I could adequately describe what I am seeing over here. The damage to this country is heartbreaking. Bridges have been bombed out . . . buildings and homes have been destroyed. There are bullet holes all over the structures that are still standing. Fire has taken a terrible toll. . . .

If the people who brought these miserable little babies into the world could only be forced to hold them and feel their little arms and legs. These little kiddies have buttocks with no more meat on them than a shinbone. But our Father in heaven loves them. . . .

I'm still looking for the children to round out the number to eight. The little fellow I want so much may not make the physical. There are lots of cute little girls but I don't allow myself to get too wrapped up in the cute, fat ones. They're the babies others will want. I want the kids that look frightened and lost. I just wish I could take all of them. . . .

All my love to all of you, Daddy.

Senator Neuberger's office sent Bertha copies of the legislation he had introduced, "A Bill for Relief of Certain Korean War Orphans." The senator requested the full names of the eight children Harry was going to bring home so they could be amended to the bill. Bertha didn't know her children's middle names yet though, so she drove to the telegraph office to write Harry.

She had used twenty-two of her twenty-two allotted words but hadn't managed to fit in the word *Love.* That would be an extra fifteen cents. After deliberating for a while, she decided Harry already knew how she felt about him, so she saved the pennies and kept the love. When she reached her car, a uniformed meter man was writing her a ticket for being a minute late.

July 3, 1955

It's ten o'clock now and the kids are all taking a nap . . . Korean style. They're all over the floor. . . .

It's a real job to make these children wear pants . . . or panties. It's much too convenient to "potty" without them. I hope we can break them of some of these habits. Many of the children in Korea simply go naked all summer long. I'm afraid that would not go so well in Creswell. . . .

It is now the morning of July fourth. Last night was the first night I stayed with the children alone. It reminded me of several years ago when some of our first six would wake us up. It is still the same. When little Paul awakened me at 2:00 AM I just knew I couldn't get up . . . but I did.

Yesterday Helen took her first step and was she proud! On the next step, however, her pride took a fall. I'm sorry you didn't get to see her. . . .

Little Judy is in a basket here on the table where I'm writing. She always kicks her feet out and gets them cold. . . .

All my love, Daddy.

As Harry cared for his sons and daughters in Korea, Bertha did all she could and prayed in Oregon. There was only one more week until the Senate adjourned, and no progress had been made.

July 22, 1955

Dear Bertha and all "The Lord giveth and the Lord taketh away. Blessed be the name of the Lord." Our little Judy went to be with the Lord last night. I have cried for her. I have prayed for her. But it was God's will to take her home. The doctor was here just the day before and he didn't think she was very sick. The nurse kept telling me she should be sent to the hospital so I sent her yesterday but it was too late. Judy was the sweetest little girl, but she was a tiny thing and we just couldn't make her grow. She never weighed more than ten pounds. . . .

Please don't work too hard haying . . . and please don't any of you get hurt. Pray for us. All my love . . .

In the morning, the telephone rang; Bertha answered, and the operator recited a telegram from Senator Neuberger: "Senate late last night unanimously passed my bill to allow you and your husband to bring eight Korean orphans to the United States. I have assurance the House of Representatives will promptly consider the legislation before adjournment. Heartiest congratulations and best wishes."

It was the last bill of the session. Passed at 11:53 PM.

The phone rang again that night. "Telegram from Congresswoman Edith Green," the operator said. "Extremely pleased to advise that Holt Bill H.R. 7043 has just been passed by the House of Representatives."

She'd done it. The farmer's wife had passed legislation through the greatest deliberative body in the world. Of the thousands of bills submitted to Congress each year, few pass and those that do pass slowly. For a personal piece of legislation like the "Holt Bill" to pass in less than two months was a political miracle.

Her family was coming home. Her eight seeds from the East.

BERTHA WOKE UP AND TUNED IN the radio to hear where Harry was and how he was doing. He and their babies were flying somewhere over the Atlantic, and the news airwaves from Portland, Oregon, to Portland, Maine, were reporting on the journey.

She arrived at the Portland International Airport in a new button-down black dress she'd bought to welcome home her growing family. A thousand spectators had got there first to glimpse history. Ten years later when landing at New York's JFK, The Beatles would only garner three times the turnout. An army of fifty cameramen and film crews mounted their equipment and rushed over to capture the expectant mother as Bertha airily walked through the terminal. Flash bulbs reflected in her wire frame glasses and questions spewed in her direction.

Through the glass wall, a Pan Am Clipper streaked across the sky and the terminal buzzed. The plane taxied to the gate, a portable ramp glided to its door, and out stepped Harry. For five historic months, she'd only had his letters. And suddenly there he was, standing in a bedraggled white short-sleeved dress shirt atop the ramp. She strode outside, climbed the stairs, and as the nation watched, kissed her husband of twenty-eight years. They ducked into the privacy of the plane and re-emerged with their family. The girls wore brightly colored silk costumes and the boys were in miniature blue jeans. All but two were barefoot. Then they squeezed into a car, which would soon be swapped for a station wagon, and drove home.

Time magazine described Bertha's appearance that night rocking a pair of babies to sleep as "a picture of contentment." She thought she looked "ancient," but it was 2:30 in the morning and she had just been delivered eight babies.

Many people who read the *Time* article criticized the Holts for adopting interracially. Harry and Bertha's decision to adopt eight Korean babies was audacious at the time not only due to the size and bi-nationality of the adoption, but because it was so blatantly public. The secrecy of adoption didn't stop with Ann Mabel Harrison on the New York City sidewalk outside the church where she was baptised. The taboo lived on through the '50s, and it was conventional for orphaned children to be matched to parents who looked like them. People were unable to fathom a family whose members loved each other but didn't look like each other. In Bertha and Harry's case, there was no pretending that a white couple in their fifties had just given birth to eight half-Asians.

Although it shocked some, the adoption inspired hundreds of other couples who wrote from every U.S. time zone asking the Holts to help them adopt a G.I. baby from Korea. Their letters were answered by the creation of Holt International Children's Services, which fifty years later is the largest international adoption agency in the world.

THE MOST RECOGNIZABLE MOTHER in the world in the early twenty-first century gained her title shortly after filming a Hollywood blockbuster about raiding tombs in khaki hot pants. During a break from shooting *Lara Croft,* Angelina Jolie visited an orphanage in Cambodia from which she would later adopt her mohawk-haired son, Maddox. When asked on CNN why she did it, the words that issued from her famous lips were simply, "I love . . ." After Maddox, she adopted Zahara, an orphan from Ethiopia whose parents had died of AIDS, and Pax, a three-year-old from Vietnam, for the same loving reason. She has used her fame for good and donated one-third of her income to global causes such as the children's nonprofit Global Action for Children, which is also where I got my first job after I finished my studies in London. According to her, she was just trying to make a small difference in the world with the "stupid" amount of money she's been paid for the work she's done.

The tattooed Angelina was not the likeliest humanitarian, but she was the latest incarnation of the long celebrity string of children's charity that stretches back to the portrait of a man in a rusty-red waistcoat framed above a hearth in Bloomsbury. The painting of Thomas Coram was painted by his close friend William Hogarth, the celebrity master of Georgian painting.

The creation of the Foundling Hospital inspired Hogarth to donate his and other artists' works to adorn the walls of the hospital. The home for children then became not only the world's first chartered charity, but the world's first public art gallery. The artwork attracted visitors to the hospital who would then deposit a few farthings in the charity box for the pleasure of seeing the paintings. Hogarth and his wife, Jane, even fostered a few of the Foundling Hospital children.

George Frideric Handel also jumped on Coram's philanthropic bandwagon; in 1749 he conducted a performance of his *Messiah* in the Foundling Hospital chapel. More than a thousand people attended, including the Prince and Princess of Wales. The concert became an annual tradition giving Handel's "Hallelujah Chorus" the renown it still enjoys in concert halls around the world each December. In all, Handel's work contributed £9,000 for the unforgotten foundlings—£1,225,000 in today's terms.

It's odd to envision a bust of Angelina Jolie sitting beside those of Hogarth and Handel. There has never been an easier game of *one-of-these-things-is-not-like-the-other.* One wanted to be a vampire "when other little girls wanted to be ballerinas." One looks great in a gun holster. One gets to kiss Brad Pitt goodnight. Despite the gaping differences between them, all three are connected by being the *it* celebrities of their era who achieved something bigger than a colossal painting, a sacred composition, a box office record. They found the simple love for a child who needed some and did their part to nudge "natural selection"—and for that, their footsteps in the progressing timeline of international adoption will be footnoted in history.

Reviewing these histories, I realized Mom and Dad had followed in those footsteps to form our family. What had started as an idea on a muddy road in London nearly 300 years ago resulted in a plane carrying my sister home to the American Midwest eighteen hours after leaving a muddy runway in India. I could link my family to history, but I still needed to rediscover my own ties to my family.

Chapter Three

AARON, BROTHER OF . . .

As a teenager, Mom swore she never wanted to have children. Then, as soon as she married Dad in her late twenties, her hormonal tide switched directions, and the only thing she wanted was to be pregnant.

There are some women who glow in pregnancy as a result of the ballooning, the attention, the bizarre miracle happening beside their bladder and intestines. Despite her maternal urges, it turned out Mom wasn't a glower. She was more of a sweater. During her nine months and three weeks of pregnancy she slept on the floor because the spring of a mattress nauseated her and triggered her round-the-clock morning sickness. At work she claims to have puked in every toilet and trashcan in Nebraska's State Capitol—men's, women's, senators', the big one with the trays on top of it in the cafeteria. So when her water finally broke, she rejoiced in agony during the fourteen hours of labor it took to get me out without an epidural. The pony-tailed doctor in Birkenstocks liked natural childbirth better. By the time Mom was in too much pain to care about what he liked, it was too late for drugs—a fact she never left out each time she told me the story of my birth.

"Jim, we're never doing this again," she told Dad. "Once I get her out of me this is it. She's going to get to be a lucky, spoiled only child."

Then the me she got wasn't the me she was expecting. All the ultrasounds and *"It's A ____!"* banners said I was a girl. Not a girl. Penis. Surprise!

Mom said she and Dad had intended to name me for my two grandfathers, who both had girls' names—Meredith and Leslie. When the doctor announced my true sex, they decided to discontinue that cruel family tradition and opened the baby name book to the crisp "Boy Names" chapter. Crunched for time, they chose the first name on the page—"*Aaron,* brother of Moses."

Mom said that before she would agree to leave the hospital, she made Dad have a vasectomy to block his swimmers so she'd never have to be pregnant again and live through another nine-plus months feeling seasick. So as I lay wrapped in a soft blue blanket in the hospital nursery, my dad lay pantsless on an operating table. I've never asked him about it because a son really needn't know everything about his father's testicles. But I suspect it's true.

Mom had a way of letting Dad know what he wanted before he had a chance to know for himself. They wouldn't have been together if she hadn't. As the story goes, Mom eyed my bearded dad across the room at a party. She had noticed him before while sharing a revolving door at the state capitol building where they both worked—she in politics, he in law. Dad had a full beard back then, thick glasses, absurdly tight jeans, and stray gray hairs raining down the back of his head.

The very first words they spoke to one another were apparently not worth remembering. Then the conversation grew into the rousing topic of raising the Nebraska state senators' salaries to $7,000 a year. Mom had been hired to lobby for the bill. Dad worked for the senator in charge of the bill's committee—the Constitutional Revision and Recreation Committee.

"I've always wondered," Mom said. "Why 'Revision' and 'Recreation'? How do those two issues go together?"

"The senator enjoys tinkering with the state constitution about as much as he likes killing animals," Dad explained. "Simple as that."

"This state never ceases to amaze me."

"I presume you aren't a native of Nebraska?"

"Oh, God no."

"Then where are you from?"

"All over the country, I guess you could say. I was a military brat growing up. But Nebraska's home for now."

"You want another drink? I'm going to get us a drink," Dad said. Then he left and when he returned with a glass in each hand, she was gone.

The next week Mom saw him walking in the hallway at work in the capitol building. "Jim dear!" she yelled down the marble corridor. "Where's my drink?"

"You would have had to stick around long enough for me to give it to you."

"So you did come back?"

"I did."

"Make it up to you Friday night? There's a fundraiser in Omaha I have to go to. Come with me?"

He did. At the end of the event they left together and made footprints in the snowy street as they went to buy a pack of cigarettes from the bowling alley across the way. The snowflakes, fat and chunky like spitballs, clung to the tips of Dad's beard. He let them be and took Mom's hand in his.

"So, you do like me," she said.

"Yes, I do."

Two years later she asked him to marry her and he repeated that same phrase.

My grandfather the chaplain (Lenore's husband) officiated at the wedding ceremony in the house on B Street my parents had bought a year before. Only Mom's parents and best friend were there to witness her blue wedding dress and Dad's brown suit. Dad's parents, who grew up on farms in South Dakota during the olden era when Mount Rushmore had only three faces, had moved to Phoenix and didn't fly in for the elopement.

Dad and Mom went to Montreal for their honeymoon. It was the most foreign place either of them had ever visited. A few years before, Mom's parents, who lived on a U.S. Air Force base in Seoul, had invited her to visit them for three weeks, but she said no because she was too afraid of flying across an ocean.

In Montreal, they sat in cafés smoking cigarettes while the bilingual waiters insisted on speaking to them in French.

"Que voulez-vous manger?"

"Sorry, we only speak English."

"Vive le Québec libre."

"Look, I know there's a revolution going on but we're American, not even Canadian. Would it be so awful to talk to us in English?"

"S'il vous plaît," Dad added.

"Retournez en Amérique."

After a week they did go home. Back to Nebraska where in 1981 about the only person you'd hear not speaking English was a Hispanic worker cutting out a cow's eyeballs in a meatpacking plant. A hundred years earlier, Nebraska had been a very multicultural state. Throngs of German and Czech and Dutch immigrants pioneered west to the prairie's greener pastures. Over time the once-separate cultures merged and now only reappear once a year at events like Germanfest, where the townspeople pull up their lederhosen and drink pints of Budweiser under the light of a full moon and a John Deere tractor's high beams.

I DON'T REMEMBER MUCH of my early years as an only child. But life was different for me then. So different that it's worth trying to recount what those few quiet years were like before my siblings came home and why the memories of that mini-era caused a frog in Dad's throat to jump through the phone when we talked about it.

My parents said I was the perfect baby. But they also said I was cute when they cut my hair in a mullet for the first four years of my life, so their judgment might not always be trustworthy.

Recalling the winter after I was born, Mom said, "it was colder than a polar bear's nose." I checked the *Farmer's Almanac.* She wasn't exaggerating. For my first Christmas, Santa brought the longest cold spell in Lincoln's recorded history—188 hours of temperatures solidly below zero degrees Fahrenheit. I was blissfully oblivious and wore three pairs of gloves each time we left the house.

My first memory—the first thing I really remember, not just know about from an almanac or photo album or Beta videocassette recorder that Dad carried on his shoulder wherever I went—is of a scratchy Halloween orange couch at the B Street house. Our chocolate lab Bunkie jumped up beside me and then that's it. End of memory. Soon after we shared the couch, Bunkie went to live on a nearby farm—not the euphemistic euthanasia kind of farm but a real one with fields and chickens. She was jealous of the new kid in the house. Plus I was told that I liked to climb up her tail expecting a ride and she didn't feel obliged.

I took inventory of Dad's videocassette catalogue to fill in the blanks of my life as an only child so I could compare them to my later existence as a big brother.

There was the orange pumpkin that took forty-five minutes for me to gut and Dad to carve one-on-one while the video camera watched and recorded. Dad must have thought we would have time in the future to sit together and watch me wipe pumpkin goo on his face without the interruption of four other siblings vying for attention.

Mom frosted my *Tyrannosaurus rex* birthday cake green and pink because as a three-year-old I was determined to become a paleontologist and couldn't get enough dinosaur paraphernalia. I knew the difference between the Triassic, Jurassic, and Cretaceous periods and the similarities between a Brachiosaurus and a Haplocanthosaurus. As an adult, now I just feel proud that I don't have to look up how to spell pterodactyl in the dictionary.

Before bed, Dad read me a section from a book he wrote especially for me titled *Pete's Pet Store Story.* "Preston and the penguin ran out of the physicians' clinic and down Peppermint Street past the photographer's studio, where a placard proclaimed: 'Our Portraits Have No Poor Traits,'" he read while I giggled. He loved to tell me stories. It was his way of forming a father-son bond with a son who had no clue how to throw a ball.

Mom's wavy waist-length hair was cut to her shoulders after she sat down on a toilet to pee and a lit votive candle behind her sent flames shooting up her back.

We drove to Colorado for Christmas with my grandparents and popped Christmas crackers at dinner. Colorful crowns and tiny toys and slips of paper flew across the table. Grandmother Lenore picked up one of the papers and read aloud a riddle about what is yellow and white and travels 80 miles per hour? "A guy with diarrhea in a racecar," Grandfather said. The real answer is still a mystery to all who were present that day.

There was one standout event that was not recorded on film but I remember the scene vividly. Each Saturday morning Dad took me to McDonald's. Just Dad and I. In the car he'd tune the dial to "99.9FM—Good Times, Great Oldies™" and we'd wait for a Beatles song to play. Or a tune by Frankie Valli and the Four Seasons. I loved those high notes.

We both ordered scrambled eggs and biscuits from the breakfast menu. "You got your salt packet?" he'd check. I liked salty eggs. He preferred pepper. The booths looked like blonde wood but were really yellow plastic in disguise.

When we were done eating we went to the hardware store. Not because he needed anything—"just browsing, thanks"—but because it made us happy. I was in love with the plunger aisle. Life didn't get much better than suctioning a plunger half my height to a tile floor and yanking it loose. It just didn't. Except of course when it was time to go home and he'd help me buckle my seatbelt in the back of his silver Buick. After making sure the strap wasn't going to slice my head off, he'd hold his hand on my shoulder. My young collarbone must have felt like a pencil case back then. While his hand relaxed there, I'd count the seconds of his affection . . . one, two, three, four.

EVEN THOUGH SHE WOULD never again endure the process of *having* any more children, when I started school, Mom was overcome by the same urge she had felt when she wanted to be pregnant. After I came out as her son, she felt the need to have a daughter so she talked Dad into adoption. In 1988, about 20,000 children awaited adoptive families in the U.S. foster care system. Most of these were older kids, and there were no guarantees with the newborns that a birth family wouldn't ask for their baby back.

It didn't matter to Mom and Dad what continent their kid came from. So on a friend's recommendation they called the Holt International adoption agency—founded by the farm family in

Oregon. The first December after the Holts adopted eight Korean orphans, with sixteen stockings hanging above the fireplace, a reporter called Bertha on her rotary phone.

"Mrs. Holt, you've been nominated for 'Mother of the Year,'" he said.

"I'm afraid I'll be too busy to be 'Mother of the Year,'" she told him before setting the phone back on the receiver and scurrying to stop one of her little ones from washing his pants in the toilet. She and Harry somehow found time to continue their mission and help other families do the same. For all her work and unprecedented motherhood, President Lyndon Johnson presented Bertha with the "National Mother of the Year" award in 1966. Harry wasn't at the ceremony. He'd died two years earlier. His overexerting love for orphans caused one final heart attack that ended his life.

Even as a widow, Grandma Bertha Holt logged up to 100,000 miles a year in her flight journals as she dined with foreign dignitaries and sat on the ground with orphans, sharing her modest love with people who did not know that a pint-sized Heidi-haired farmer's wife from Oregon could care so much. When the new millennium dawned, Grandma died too. She was laid to rest in a lavender *hanbok* and running shoes beside her husband on a hill in Korea where they built their first orphanage.

In 1988, when I was five, Mom and Dad set up an appointment with Holt in Omaha for them to meet with one of the adoption agency's social workers.

"Do you recognize this place?" Dad told me he asked Mom once he had parked and they started walking across the street. A bowling alley was on the other side.

"Yeah. Wow. Weird. This is where we went to get cigarettes on our first date."

Dad took Mom's hand in his. "No snow this time."

Inside the agency's office, which was in the building beside Lucky Lanes, their social worker, Cathy, gave my parents a pile of paperwork to fill out to apply for a child—the little girl they were meant to have five years earlier, before I came out with a few extra parts. One section of the application asked fifty-five questions for them to answer separately. Mom wrote hers in swoopy cursive when she got home. Dad used a typewriter.

"Jim and I are a study in opposites," she wrote. *"I am gregarious, extroverted, talkative, assertive, temperamental, impatient and fun loving. Jim is shy, introverted, quiet, indecisive, patient and witty. We are both very kind and loving, respectful of others and we complement each other. Generally, we interpret the world and events in the same way."*

Then Dad:

> *"I am quiet, introverted, and not prone to make quick decisions. Deb is talkative, extroverted, and impulsive. We seem to complement each other quite well."*

The next section of the application tested just how daring they were willing to be. It asked them to check "Yes," "No," or "Maybe" on a list of special medical needs. Would they consider adopting a child with a congenital hip defect? A heart defect? Physical disfigurement, allergies, or sex-change surgery? Webbed feet, cerebral palsy, blind, deaf, diabetes, hemophilia, cleft palate, burns? The answer to each was "No." The two pages were a solid column of negative checkmarks except for a "Maybe" beside birthmark.

They wanted a healthy baby to complete their picture-perfect father-mother-daughter-son American family. But when it came to family planning, my parents' expectations never matched what they got. Just compare my bubble-less bath videos to my ultrasound pictures for proof that if they weren't so blinded by the love of a parent, they should have seen the shock coming when it came to each of their children.

My sister liked to hear the story of the first time Mom and Dad found out about her.

"Hello?"

"Deb, this is Cathy," my parents' social worker said.

"Hi Cathy! You calling with good news?"

"I think so. How insistent are you and Jim on having a perfectly healthy girl?"

"Well, it depends. How serious are we talking?"

"I have paperwork for a little girl in India with some slight birth defects."

"I think we can do slight. I'll check with Jim but slight should be alright."

"Great! I'll mail you all the information then."

Dad opened the referral letter a couple of days later. "Here's our girl, Deb." He showed her the photograph. An Indian baby's brown eyes looked deep into the camera. She had wild black hair and a little tongue that poked out to the left.

Then more pictures started to arrive. They were close-ups of the "slight" birth defects. Scarred ankles that looked as if a rubber band had been wrapped around them for weeks. Fingers that were stuck together. Toes that would never have toenails.

And then the video arrived. It was filmed in a mint-green medical room and featured an Indian doctor wearing a stethoscope around his neck and a white shirt that reflected the wall color. Babies cried in the background.

"This is Kirti," he said. "She was brought to us on the seventh day of life, three and a half months back. She was born with multiple abnormalities to a mother who was very short. When I saw her first she had skin infection. She had jaundice. Was looking very frail."

The infant on the examination table gazed into the doctor's face.

"We can find the abnormalities on the fingers and the toes. This is a fusion of the fingers." The camera zoomed in to his hand holding hers. One of the doctor's fingernails was the size of her entire palm. He flicked at the nub of flesh above the point where her two fingers combined. "There had been one more fingertip that was tied up too, but it appears to have already fallen."

The camera panned down to the baby's foot. "And this here is all joined toes. And a band on her ankle." The doctor picked her up and held her like a football. "Spine seems to be OK. Seems to be very alert and active. She smiles a lot," he said looking into the camera just as the baby began to cry.

End of video.

My sister didn't hear the end of the story she loved so much until recently.

"Jim?" Mom asked.

No answer. He went quiet for a week. Dad was always a quiet guy, but this was a new record.

Finally one night at dinner he spoke. "She's still our girl, Deb."

"I know that. I was just waiting for you to, too."

Chapter Four

THE CIRCUS OF LIFE

AROUND THE TIME I WAS POTTY-TRAINING, my two oldest siblings were born in India—Michelle about three years before Jordan. Back then they were known as Ganga and Bhola. They lived with their parents in a one-room shanty made from birds' nest materials until their father died, possibly of stomach cancer. After he was gone, their mom left them alone to fend for themselves when she went to work.

Baby Jordan ran around the village naked most of the time. Michelle had long black hair, thick like a horse's tail. When she was younger, she also had a bad case of chicken pox that left dime-sized divots on her skin where they had become infected.

Although she was younger than five, Michelle remembered a gang of monkeys that attacked her and Jordan in their shanty one night when their mom was out working. To escape, Michelle kicked through the mud wall of her house and tugged baby Jordan out to safety. Jordan did not remember the attack, but as a result of it he was scared to be in the same room with an animal until after he reached puberty. It took our family a ballistic encounter between Jordan and a poodle for Michelle to share this horror story and reveal an ounce of the ocean of complexities they carried with them from India. She had told this story and others into a tape recorder at an Indian police station the week before she and Jordan were sent to the orphanage.

Worse foes than monkeys attacked them when they were home alone. But Michelle was not so forthright recounting these tales. She couldn't be. Her mind had repressed them, and she would not remember until a decade after she had lost her Indian accent.

When he was still an infant, Jordan was kidnapped for his unusually light skin color. An Indian's worth is still often valued by the lightness of his or her skin today, but it was an even bigger prize for a boy in 1980s India. The adults who took Jordan planned to raise him as their own in the hope that his upper-caste skin hue would bring him and them success in the future; at that time, lighter skin meant more opportunities for education and employment.

Somehow, beyond Michelle's memory, their Indian mom tracked down Jordan's whereabouts on her own. But the only leverage she had to get her son back was to offer to exchange the virginity of Michelle, her five- or six-year-old daughter, to his captors as a barter. It's unthinkable, but like so many untouchable women in India without a living husband or a government that cared to protect the underclass, she was powerless. She only had two options: Michelle or Jordan. In the end, Jordan was saved and Michelle was sacrificed.

BRITISH AIRWAYS FLIGHT 143 touched down at 23:37 military time at the Indira Gandhi International Airport in New Delhi. Earlier that morning, I had handed in the key to my room at Goodenough College, walked by the gate to Coram's Field, and begun my journey to the places where my brother and sisters got their start and their scars. I needed to discover how they got around, what they ate, who else lived in their neighborhood, where they slept, and what noises woke them up in the middle of the night. I also wanted to visit their orphanages, meet the people who cared for them, and get to know the kids who were not adopted. These experiences, the details that my siblings couldn't remember and that I could never know without living them myself, were the keys to getting back in with my family again.

Just days before I flew, I had finished my final exams at The London School of Economics where I was studying for a degree in globalization. On my first day of class a year before, I had given myself a few extra minutes in the morning to make sure that my long bangs, which grew to my eyebrows like a Beatle's, were swept to the side just so. I slipped into a pair of designer jeans and stepped outside. My clickity-clack black shoes brushed the falling orange leaves of Coram's Field as I passed Virginia Woolf's property, Charles Dickens's pub, Amy Winehouse's police station.

On that first day of class I arrived at the urban campus fifteen minutes before 11:00 and sat in one of fifteen seats in a tall room with broad tables. Our professor, who looked uncomfortably as if he were related to Austin Powers, had assigned his book *The Global Transformations Reader* so I unloaded it from my army-green bag and waited, ready. But at 11:08 when the professor asked me if I thought a rigorous conception of globalization could be defended, I realized I had no idea what I was doing there.

I had to work for that degree. I got through it though with the help of some much smarter coursemates, £17 in library fines, and weekly summits at the George IV campus pub. As summer rolled around and I began to pack for my world tour, I thought again, "I'm ready." I knew what I was doing. I was a Master in the ways of the modern globalized world.

As I strolled onto the gangway between the British Airways airplane and the Indian airport, I choked on the hot wet, gritty air. I knew that smell—it was reminiscent of the vapors that cleared my sinuses when I'd first caught a whiff of my sister Michelle's hair a few minutes after she had landed in the States. Even though the odor and I were old acquaintances, I had never been introduced to how the smell felt to inhale in July on the opposite side of the planet. It was like standing over a pot of boiling saffron and sulfur. I had adjusted my Velcro wristwatch to almost midnight, but it felt like two o'clock in the afternoon on the hottest day of my life.

Four khaki-clad officers with rifles monitored the customs queue. They were still and expressionless like the stuffed wolves at a natural history museum. I distracted myself from the guns by looking up at the fishing net that caught debris from the crumbling ceiling. The net was suspended over the heads of the customs officials—aging men with tufts of hair that appeared to have been dyed with a packet of cherry Kool-Aid. I presented my passport and visitor visa and for half a second hoped to be refused entry and flown back to an airport with intact ceilings and deodorant. "Welcome to India," the Kool-Aid–headed customs official said as he handed back my passport. I was in.

As my lungs struggled to filter oxygen inside Delhi's airport, I was weighed down by a reality I had never read about in *The Global Transformations Reader* and that I never could have comprehended in my childhood. Back then, the early chapters of Michelle and Jordan's lives on the streets of India had always resembled a Chagall painting in my mind. The surreal events they recounted swirled around the canvas like a goat playing the cello for a bride dressed in red. The odd incidents of monkey attacks and kidnappings stood out amid the foggy surroundings but I couldn't make sense of them. Their memories were too far out of my world for me to understand.

But this was the air they breathed. The land they knew as home. This is where their journeys had begun.

I retrieved my bag from the carousel. It was a small blue roll-on jam-packed with a color wheel of solid T-shirts, waterproof sandals, bug spray, anti-diarrhea pills, and enough pairs of underwear to get me by in case the pills didn't work. I gripped the suitcase's handle and approached the arrivals gate, where a thousand people awaited me. Half the crowd were standing behind the metal rail barrier holding signs in scribbled English, Sanskrit, and Spanish that spelled the names of other foreign travelers. The other 500 people were strewn around the room wherever they fit. Women in saris and bangles slept on the window ledges. Men in Sikh turbans squatted on the green-gray slate floor. A few nimble teenagers attached their small sleeping bodies to the metal rails like spiders in a web.

Hands clamored to help me with my luggage—the skin that touched mine was so rough that it didn't have a temperature. I assured the many men and boys who wanted to help me that I had everything under control. "Under control" did not translate in Punjabi. I gave in to a man in his early thirties who said the magic words, "I get you out here."

He whisked me into a parking lot that looked like a desert junkyard for white Hondas. The man put my bag in the trunk of one of the Hondas and shoved me into the back. A well-fed fourteen-year-old was in the driver's seat. His name was Tui, "like the bird," he added. Tui turned on the ignition and with a gassy jolt that startled the Ganesha bobble-head on the dash, we were moving. The Honda's dim fog lights illuminated the ten feet in front of the car. I asked Tui why no other vehicles were using headlights. "Why need light? We have honk," he said in a squeaky voice and added his own to the car horn symphony playing on National

Highway 8. For the next hour we drove like this, like trumpeting bats in the urban night.

When it came to lanes, Tui did not discriminate. Most other drivers considered the dotted line down the middle at least a polite suggestion, but Tui accepted it as an invitation to straddle the whole road. He specialized in jerking the car aside at the last instant when he heard the honking blast of a truck without headlights that was heading right at us. The swerving was so severe that at times I thought the Ganesha doll's rattling elephant head might bobble off. I shifted to the middle of the back seat, away from the doors. A pack of wild brown dogs dashed across the road like deer.

I looked at young Tui in the rearview mirror and counted the seconds his eyes were rested. He averaged four seconds closed for every one open. I shook his shoulder. "Hey!" I screamed. "You like music?" He dug through the sheets of crinkled paper in the glove compartment for a black cassette tape. He stuck it into the stereo system. A banshee cry filled the car and he sang along to the allegro song from an old Bollywood movie probably filmed before he was born. *Dekha Ek Khwaaaaaaab.*

At 2:00 AM we pulled into the drive of the Maidens Hotel, a white colonial building fortified with a 15-foot concrete fence. Tui opened the trunk and I saw my bag. I ran to it, pulled it out like a baby from a bassinet and held out my hand to Tui to shake. Instead of taking it, Tui clasped both of his together like a church choirboy in prayer, tipped his head, and said, "Namasté."

"Namasté," I echoed, remembering the word my economics professor greeted us with at the start of every lesson.

A doorman in a red suit held open a giant glass door and I passed through into the marble foyer. As the door glided shut, I looked over my shoulder at the four-wheeled white blur swerving around the piles of people and rubble lying on the side of the street.

"Where were you?" my to-be travel companion NASA-Jeff asked when he opened the door to room 305.

"With Tui," I said.

NASA-JEFF FLICKED ON THE LIGHT three hours later.

"Already?" I asked and sat up on the cot.

"Already."

The bumpy road to the Taj Mahal was 115 miles long. Our driver said the journey would take five hours so "we need early start." There were four of us who met in the hotel lobby at five o'-clock in the morning. We knew each other from London where we had all been American students living abroad. For individual reasons, we had each decided to spend our summer vacations traveling in India, and we synced our plans so we could reunite for this ride.

Still too terrified to be tired, I sat on a bench in the back of the jeep next to Legs, a tall blonde from Kansas with a fever for hip-hop and public health. She was in India investigating the lives of gay male Indian sex workers whose wives either did not know or pretended not to know what they did each night when they were out of the house. Legs's other Indian incentive was her Indian boyfriend who also lived there. She was living with him, but that was a bigger secret than the married gay prostitutes'. NASA-Jeff was beside her in his signature ball cap. He thumbed through his passport, for which he'd had to send away for more pages because he traveled so often. NASA-Jeff's goal in life was to be the first man on Mars. India seemed like a natural first step. Then there was PopTart, a child-rights advocate who had just escaped a three-day gunfight outside her hotel in the ethnically divided streets of Kashmir, 500 miles west of Delhi, where she was doing a summer internship. Now she was popping up and down in the front seat like the five-foot-two sparkler she is.

Besides bumpy, the road to the Taj Mahal was also bumper-to-bumper with hundreds of thousands of white jeeps, auto rickshaws, buses, lorries, walkers, and loafing cows who were the undisputed kings of the road. The side of our jeep doors spelled *TOURIST* in blue letters so big NASA-Jeff said space satellites could read it from Mars but not Saturn. It didn't really matter how many light-years it took before the word lost its legibility. In this year, on this day, it was beckoning every highway peddler for miles to us like flies to the fire. Most of the peddlers knew only a few words of English, but they all recognized the shape of the word *TOURIST* and the color of our hair when they peered through the windows at us.

In the stalled traffic the peddlers came and tapped on our windows with red fingernails, stained from wadding up the fiery addictive chew that sustained their days. They hawked whatever they had that day—bangles, chai tea, used Fruit of the Loom undershirts. "Three chai," PopTart said and handed a man a few rupees through the window.

A man in a loose white robe crouched in the sand beside a short basket on the side of the road. He withdrew a musical recorder from a hidden pouch in his shirt, removed the basket's lid, and put his lips to the instrument. A black cobra shimmied in the dusty dawn. "No. Fucking. Way," Legs said, punctuating each word. "That's not really supposed to work, is it?" The cobra was three feet vertical and was fanning the scales of its neck like a devil peacock. The man tucked the recorder back into his robes and lifted the snake high until I made contact with its red eyes through the window. Then, on the owner's command, it pounced at the glass and I shrieked. Lowercase letters don't do my embarrassment justice. I *SHRIEKED.*

"Buck up, Eske," PopTart said, turning around in her seat to see my face. "Your nerves will get used to it soon. As soon as you get to know it."

"Used to snakes jumping at my face?"

"You'll be used to way worse by the time you fly outta here."

"Oh joy."

No one outside our car could have heard my snake wail. It merely merged with the sound of the eternal highway honking. I faced forward to see a carnival-colored lorry truck taking 800 caged chickens to market. A single wood plank held the cages in place and on it were three words painted in hot orange that barked the phrase, "HONK. OK. PLEASE." Every lorry we passed had those three words painted on its rear, and as we passed them, we honked. As did all the other drivers on the road . . . OK . . . Please.

Stalled in the traffic beside us was a green striped bus that looked as if it could have dropped my grandparents off on their first day of school. Brown hands and black hair stuck out from its barred windows, reaching for fresh air. Thirty or so men with 26-inch waists sat tightly on top of the bus, and five more clung to the ladder on back.

"Would you rather be on top or inside the bus?" I asked the passengers of the air-conditioned jeep.

"On top."

"Top."

"I never thought I'd say this, but on top of the bus. Yeah, definitely top."

We couldn't agree so easily about which part of the auto rickshaw we'd rather squeeze into. An "auto" is a riding lawn mower with three wheels and a springy park bench glued down in back. A yellow pleather flap covers the top of most of them to shield the occupants from the rain but there are no doors or windows to keep its exhaust fumes from turning your lungs into gas chambers. Three people and a driver can ride an auto rickshaw comfortably enough. Through our windshield PopTart counted eighteen people in the auto directly ahead of us. I could only see seventeen, but that's because "there's a kid down by the pedals," she added.

"That's where I'd want to be," I said. "I'd punch down the brakes and walk the rest of the way."

"What if they're going all the way south to Bangalore?" NASA asked.

"All the more reason to get out."

"I'd be more comfortable anywhere in there compared to sitting up here with all this space while they stare at me," PopTart said. She had a point. Four women riding backward and sitting in the auto rickshaw's back luggage bin gazed at her with a uniform expression—the sum of loathing and lethargy—as they bounced down the highway.

A few miles later our driver pulled over and left us and the car with the keys and without a word. We sat in silence, wondering to ourselves. A larger man trudged along the shoulder of the road toward us. Two metal chains connected his clenched fists to the necks of a pair of langur monkeys that trailed their captor. "Ten rupees says they stop at our car," NASA said. They did.

The langurs, big as baboons with whips for tails, began to do back flips in the dirt. I had heard of them. They were just like the monkeys Michelle had described—the ones that broke into her house. Their fur was tan like sand and their faces were human-like, villainous humans.

I bent down to reach for my bottle of water. The car was starting to bake without the air conditioning. I sat back up and looked out the window, expecting to see more primate aerobics outside. Instead, I saw the flaring nostrils of a langur, perched on the window ledge three inches from my face. I *SHRIEKED again.*

"Still not used to it, eh, Eske?"

"I know why Jordan doesn't like animals."

"What?"

"My brother Jordan . . . zoophobia. Never mind, it's not important," I said, even though it meant more than I could say.

The langur tapped its fingernails on the glass. They clicked like needles in a tattoo parlor. Legs took a picture of the monkey and me. In the photograph, my mouth was open in the kind of horrified smile you see on video monitors at the end of a roller coaster ride.

When Legs's camera flashed, the langur hopped off the window and patted his master's leg. The man walked toward PopTart's front door and gestured for her to roll down her window as if he was a traffic cop. She rolled it one inch. "Monkey say you take picture. Six hundred rupees," he ordered.

"No, sir. The monkey did not tell you we took a picture," PopTart said and rolled up her window.

"Yes he say! You pay me 600 rupees!" The glass could not muffle his anger.

PopTart shook her head. His hand reached for her door handle and her fingers scurried for the lock. He was faster. This time I was not the only person to *SHRIEK*. PopTart tugged the door closed but he had wedged his wrist inside.

"You pay 500 rupees!" he yelped while wagging his fingers inside the jeep.

"No! Move your arm!" PopTart shouted back. She was still holding the door firm, crushing his hand. "Where's our driver?!" The chained langurs jumped onto the windows again. They tapped.

"Four hundred rupees!" he bargained. The langurs tapped faster.

"PopTart, I took a picture," Legs said. "Here's 300." She leaned into the front seat and tucked the pink notes into the man's palm. At Travelex currency exchange, 300 rupees would get you $6. In rural India, it would buy 30 simple meals. He stopped struggling, and PopTart relieved some pressure. Then the man walked away with the money and without a word, back to wherever he and his trailing langurs had come from. We sat in wondering silence once more and stayed that way even after the driver returned with a vegetable samosa, which he nibbled on as he turned the key in the ignition.

A few hours later we arrived at the gravel parking lot a mile from the Taj Mahal—cars weren't allowed any nearer because the cultural conservationists were worried that smog would tarnish the national treasure. To get to the Taj grounds, you could either walk or hire a camel with bleeding feet to pull you in the cart he was chained to. As we walked, a pack of children selling Taj Mahal snow globes in the 100-degree heat escorted us halfway.

PopTart walked up ahead and passed through the Taj gates first. When I caught up to her, she was staring down at the empty reflecting pool and up at the most recognizable tomb in the world, built by an emperor for the love of his life.

"It's like I forgot the man with the monkeys was human," she said. "Maybe I'm too used to it."

The drive back to Delhi was dark. The "HONK. OK. PLEASE" lorries were decked in strings of every-color lights as they rolled along the highway like a fleet of trailer homes on Christmas Eve. A moped with seven heads and fourteen feet passed us. The dad was steering the two-wheeler, mom straddled dad, grandma straddled her, a newborn was strapped to grandma's back, two toddlers clung to their mother's breasts, and a standing eight-year-old held on to the handlebar, helping his father steer.

"Look, it's a goddamn clown show," Legs said.

"YOU EVER BEEN TO DANS LE NOIR?" NASA-Jeff asked me while he and I were waiting on the platform for our overnight train to take us away from the millennium-old temples of Khajuraho.

"Dawn la what?" I asked back. "NASA, if that's French then I never learned it. I don't even know how to say, 'I don't speak French,' in French."

NASA chuckled a polite *haha* as he did every time I thought I was being funny. The habit was a little disingenuous but I didn't mind. "It's the blind restaurant. They turn off the lights while you eat so you can't see your food. Like you're eating blind."

"You going to open one on this train station platform? Because you could."

Haha.

He really could have, though. It was blindingly dark. The electricity at the Jhansi railway station had cut out a few minutes earlier as part of North India's routine and unannounced rolling blackouts. From what I could hear, none of the other masses of people clustered on Platform 3 so much as flinched when the lights were extinguished. The rumble of 10,000 voices, footsteps, and whistles kept on keeping on. The only difference my ears could discern in the dark was the missing sound of light. I didn't know how soothing the hum of 10,000 volts was until it was zapped, and I was surrounded by all that natural, eerie noise.

SHORTLY AFTER JORDAN WAS RECLAIMED from his kidnappers and reunited with Michelle, their mom fell ill with tuberculosis. Hoping for a miracle, she led her children on a pilgrimage to Shirdi, a small holy town in central India that is known throughout India for being the birthplace of Sai Baba, the guru of charity.

For days they rode on top of a train car to get there, ducking for tunnels and holding on to each other during a turn in the tracks. Michelle slept atop the white sack that contained everything her family owned in the world. Almost all of the bag's contents had originally been stolen by Michelle and her birth mother, so it was purely cruel karma when the white sack was stolen from underneath her while she slept. They arrived in Shirdi with nothing.

I TURNED TO NASA, who was rubbing his eyes.

"Funny seeing you here," he said.

"Not for long." The caboose passed us and our world was black again.

"Did you see the front page of the *Times of India* today?" he asked.

"Nope."

"I'd get it out and show you, but . . ."

I nodded as if my movements mattered. I could have stripped off all my clothes and done jumping-jacks on the train tracks and no one would have known. It was so black that even the moon was afraid to come out from behind the clouds. All that was visible were a few ember red cigarette butts tangoing in space like fireflies.

"So, this guy in the paper was riding in the back of an auto rickshaw and got impaled by a flying pole. Right through his gut. There was a picture."

"How awful," I said. "Did he die instantly?"

"No, that's the thing. He sat there pinned. Waited 90 minutes with a pole piercing his ribs thinking someone would come by to rescue him. When nobody did, *then* he got out his cell phone and called his family for help."

"What, did he get bored waiting to die?"

"Maybe he thought he already had and that was his afterlife."

The thought of being pinned to an auto rickshaw for eternity made me shudder. "Reincarnate me as a cow already."

The rising pitch of a train whistle approached. The locomotive slowed and stopped in front of us, lighting the platform in fluorescent shadows. Women carrying white bags on their heads scurried to the nearest door as if playing a game of musical chairs. Hundreds of bodies in stained clothing rose from the ground like zombies from the grave and writhed their way to the platform edge. Those who could reach placed their hands on the blue steel train, staking their claim. Only so many people could fit inside. Everyone else would have to ride on top.

The sliding doors thundered open and in each blazing frame appeared the silhouette of a guard waving a meter stick at the hundred-man scrums below. Every hand on the train drummed the steel. The men's howls soared above the guards' whistling. The guards' sticks beat the doorframes like a dinner triangle and they lashed the men like mules. Yet the people on the platform fought forward in their dogged scramble. To think they were fighting for the chance to ride a thousand miles on a wooden bench alongside however many other humans were able to squeeze in the train car.

"Humanity's a zoo."

"Claws your soul, huh."

"I wish it was dark again."

The train cars were so brimming with people that the open doors began vomiting bodies.

Farther down the platform a pair of young women raced toward their reserved train car, for which they had paid $9 more. The beading on their matching pink saris shimmered in the train light as they ran. The train whistle bellowed its "all aboard" blow. The taller woman jumped onto the train and when she looked over her shoulder at her friend who had fallen behind, she saw her crumpled on the platform. She'd run into the long handle of a wheelbarrow and was clutching her winded diaphragm. She wasn't moving. The train wheels turned on the tracks and the women stared at each other in the growing obscurity, powerless to utter a word.

"If you dare do that to me—leave me here—there will be an assassin waiting for you at Heathrow," I said.

Haha.

"I'm not joking, NASA. I will personally hire the top hit man in Britain."

~

ONCE MICHELLE, JORDAN, AND THEIR mother arrived in Shirdi with nothing but each other and the clothes on their backs, they went to Sai Baba's temple. They had traveled there not only to worship but also to live alongside the hundreds of other untouchable families who, like them, were hoping for a little charity.

For about a year, their mother tried earning some money by cooking for the wealthier villagers. Michelle, age six or seven, earned the rest by begging for money on the street outside the white and gold temple, all the while responsible for taking care of baby Jordan. When she wasn't begging, she made Diwali candles to sell to temple-goers. Sometimes men would give her food or candy out of generosity. And sometimes they'd give her food or candy in exchange for having sex with them.

Like her dying mother, Michelle too was sick with tuberculosis and had *the* cough. And like almost every other street child, she went to bed itching when the bumpy scabies under her skin began to move around as they laid a fresh batch of eggs.

When Michelle and Jordan's mother died outside Sai Baba's temple, her corpse was disposed of like a black garbage bag piled up on a New York City street corner. They had no known relatives and at six and two years old, their survival was placed in Michelle's hands—the outstretched hands of a girl with a full set of permanent teeth and a pair of big, old, knowing, needing eyes.

~

I CROSSED PATHS WITH LEGS AGAIN in monsoon Mumbai a couple weeks after parting from NASA-Jeff. Legs had warned me about the city's lidless manholes before I had even packed for the round-the-world journey.

"You'll be wet to your knees walkin' along and then slurp—you're swirlin' in like a wedding ring down the goddam drain," she'd said.

Apparently, manhole lids were handy things to have around the house so people stole them. And in a place where houses were constructed with bed sheet roofs and billboard walls like the one Michelle and Jordan used to live in, I could believe it.

So, as Legs and I walked hand-in-hand in Mumbai through the roads-cum-Venetian-canals in the pouring rain, I stared down at the brown floodwater engulfing my ankles. Only part of me truly thought my next step would be my last, but I was not taking any chances. Whenever I mustered the courage to glance upward, the world was a bleary streak of oversized black and rainbow umbrellas. We didn't have an umbrella. I had packed a thick argyle sweater instead in case of a cold spell. It was 110 degrees, a bubbling 212 with humidity. A salty cocktail of sweat and rain rolled down my overgrown hair and into my eyeballs as I kept gazing downward, searching for would-be whirlpools.

"Have you seen any yet?"

"Any what?" Legs asked.

"Whirlpools?"

"Like the bathtub?"

"No. Whirlpools . . . vortexes in the water. You know, the telltale sign of a missing manhole."

"Is that really the telltale sign?"

"I don't know. I figured so."

"You look out for whirlpools, I'll look for the nose-piercer."

I kept watching the water like Legs said to so she could find the man we heard about who would pierce her nose. When the falling raindrops, some as big as almonds, shattered the water surface, I expected to see a splashing crown, the split-second-triple-back-twist Olympic Greg Louganis kind. Or at least to feel a little backsplash on my upper shins when the rain made contact with the earth. But the current was so strong, it sucked the raindrop in without much fanfare and sped ahead.

"I can't believe you're going through with this," I said.

"Getting my nose pierced?"

"Yeah, on the street in Mumbai."

"It's just a souvenir."

"Does tetanus count as a souvenir?"

"If it comes with a pretty gem on top then it does."

"My sister Michelle came home with a pierced nose. Her mom gave it to her when she was still a baby. But when she came to America she refused to wear the nose ring. She didn't think it fit her new American lifestyle."

"Did the hole close when she took out the ring?"

"Yeah, until she jabbed a safety pin back into it during math class in junior high."

"Fuck me that musta hurt."

"You're about to find out."

The current below grew stronger. I burrowed my toes into the soles of my rubber sandals, afraid of one running away in the stream. They were all that separated my water-pruned feet and the rutted market road.

"Dee-ah-monds for your wife," a merchant called out to me from within his tin-hatched hut. He clutched a string of rhinestones that on a sunny day would have reflected the many colors of Mumbai. Today, however, the monsoon had water-colored the whole city brown.

"Oh, he's not my husband," Legs replied and released my hand from hers. I used it to wring out the rain from my green linen shirt in vain and then reached for her grip once more. If I ended up tumbling down a manhole on her quest for a nose piercing, then she was coming along for the ride. I figured drowning in a pipe of human waste was surely best experienced with a friend anyway.

"Dee-ah-monds for your mee-stress then," the merchant persisted.

"Oh, he doesn't work like that," she assured him.

I tugged Legs away but there was no escaping the chorus pouring from the endless row of shop stalls that was heavier than the rain. "Very nice inside," they all yelled from under the candy-cane-striped awnings that kept them dry. It wasn't every day that a pair of white (rich) travelers happened upon Mumbai's wholesale jewelry bazaar. Especially not in the middle of the July deluge.

Legs and I were both used to the weather elements though, having grown up in the Midwest's tornado alley. What we weren't so accustomed to were the daggered stares of a thousand strangers who were all shocked to see a man and a woman touching skins in public. So I kept my head down, determined to know what was coming and not know who was caring that I was a white man in the wrong neighborhood and was holding a woman's hand.

A drowned rat drifted past. Then an empty pack of cigarettes and a red Coca-Cola can written in what I thought resembled Punjabi but that Legs said might have been Marathi.

"The difference is all in the bindis," she said, expecting me to know what she was talking about. I didn't.

A tangerine bouquet of prayer flowers swathed Legs's ankle, and I became conscious of the tinkling temple bells and coughingly sweet incense that was wafting in our direction through the steam particles of the storm. She knelt down, gently picked up the floating bouquet, and draped it ceremoniously around my neck. Despite being awash in sludge, the flowers' soft petals smelled fresh, almost clean. I parted the sopping black hair from my eyes and admired the delicate talisman.

"I love it," I said. And I did. "This is my kind of souvenir."

We rounded the corner and there, polishing his needles in the rain atop the yellow passenger seat of a bicycle rickshaw, was the man we had come to see. Legs waded over to him and he stood taller, using his thumb to casually brush off the dewy drips from his thin black moustache.

"Hello tio," she said, filing away her Midwest way and speaking in what could only be described as Kwik-E-Mart English inspired by *The Simpsons*. At home, amongst my siblings, I would have found the accent insulting. After two weeks of trying to communicate in India, I'd learned to respect it. "You pierce my nose, no?" she asked.

"OK. OK," he answered. Gathering his sharp tools he told Legs her beautiful (white) skin would look "most bee-you-tee-fool" dotted with an "ee-merald."

As the longer-than-you-would-expect needle approached Legs's nostril, she at first crossed her eyes to watch. But before it struck, she clenched her eyelids closed and squeezed my hand, which she was still holding. We felt the needle's pinch together—in her nose, on my fingers. A fine bead of ruby blood bubbled beside the emerald stone and then an almond raindrop rinsed it away.

"Oh, thank you, tio," she said and fingered her Caribbean coin purse for rupees.

We turned to retrace our steps. Or at least to retrace them as best we could considering that the originals were all submerged in muck. Emboldened by the knowledge that we had not yet been eaten by a manhole and slightly amused by the thought of it, I blinkingly glanced up to the hellish heavens, opened my mouth in a smile, and drank in India.

Chapter Five

A SEED IN THE MUD

It was the watchman at the Sai Baba temple who turned Michelle and Jordan—Ganga and Bhola—over to the Shirdi police after their mom died. He was just a kid himself, but he had seen the short futures of enough children like Michelle and Jordan to know they weren't going to make it on their own.

So after years on the street, they were off. But they were still orphaned. The authorities tried to trace Michelle and Jordan's surviving relatives by speaking with people in the community, airing pictures of them on TV, and printing pictures of them in the newspaper. When no family came forward, they were moved to the Bharatiya Samaj Seva Kendra (BSSK) orphanage in Pune under the care of Mrs. Joshi, the director.

Their heads were sheared to remove the parasites that lived in their hair. Michelle pleaded with them to let her keep her hair, which covered most of her back, but it had to go. Michelle was also started on treatment for her tuberculosis.

BSSK was a muddy two-story brick building that would have made a lovely colonial estate 100 years before. The engravings on the banisters and the teal paint on the walls had chipped and faded. What had once been the front yard was now a highway overpass, under which families dwelled in makeshift tents. Inside the orphanage, one faucet served as dual dishwasher and shower. The infants slept six to a crib. The older children slept on the floor up against the wall. For Michelle and Jordan, it must have been luxury. Yet they still lacked a family. Just one month before Michelle and Jordan arrived at BSSK, Mrs. Joshi had hugged our baby sister Meredith goodbye. She was flying away to her new home in Nebraska. Despite my future siblings' almost crossing paths, they would have to wait another two years to live together.

On the day of her departure, a single red *bhindi* dot balanced between Meredith's eyebrows to protect her on the flight to Lincoln, Nebraska. She was born Kirti, the 3.8-pound daughter of an unmarried fifteen-year-old dwarf. Her mother would have been disowned by her family and disqualified from future marriages if anyone had discovered her pregnancy. So she kept it a secret and hid in a birthing shelter for women in her same situation. The clinic was overcrowded and struggled to be sanitary, but at least it was safer than exile.

At ten months and thirteen pounds, Kirti left BSSK and became Meredith Leslie, my first sister. While Meredith settled into her new home with me in Lincoln, Nebraska, Michelle and Jordan adjusted to theirs in Pune, India. Jordan's orphanage admissions paperwork described his "round innocent face with black expressive eyes and black hair." He also had a round belly, which was full from hunger, not food. Due to the lack of protein in his diet, Jordan was sick with kwashiorkor, which caused his gut to balloon with inflamed fluid.

During the first week at the orphanage, 3-foot 1-inch Jordan clung to his big (3-foot 5-inch) sister, but he gradually made friends with the other children like Aslam and Mohan. The dialect the nurses and other children spoke in BSSK was different from the language he had grown up learning. To get by, even when he knew the words, Jordan talked via hand signals. Hands weren't the only body part Jordan gestured with to get what he wanted. When he was caught being mischievous, which was often, he fired his secret weapon—a disarmingly innocent smile—and escaped trouble.

Michelle, whose paperwork described her as a "happy and smiling child" was one of BSSK's oldest children, even though they were not sure of her exact age. Orphans in India were not eligible for international adoption if they were older than six, so that's how old Michelle was. On her own she liked to play with a set of Hindu deity dolls. The gods with multiple arms and elephant heads were carved from wood and painted in pastel. They were hers as long as she was at BSSK. When she left, she'd have to leave them for the next child.

During group time (which at the orphanage was almost all the time), Michelle helped the younger children get dressed, but she always looked out for Jordan in particular. She'd raised him this far and wasn't inclined to stop at BSSK. He was her only family so she personally ensured that he ate his chapatti bread, vegetables, rice, and lentil soup at dinner and drank his glass of milk for breakfast.

AMIDST THE TAJ MAHAL AND rainy jewelry bazaars, my main mission in India was to visit BSSK. The new BSSK building that was constructed a few years after my siblings moved to Nebraska was a five-story white cement tower with criss-cross bars on its four-paneled windows. I climbed the white marble steps of the new center and heard the scraping of fifty spoons on metal breakfast bowls. A youthful woman in a gold and green sari was walking down the steps, and we met mid-flight. "Namasté," I said and bowed. "Where is Roxana?"

"You are Ganga-Bhola's big brother?"

"Yes."

"I knew so. I was waiting. I was Ganga-Bhola's nurse at the old building. Are they well?"

"Wow," was the only word I could articulate through my awe. "Uhm, yeah, they are well . . . Wow."

"Roxana is on floor four."

"Thanks," I bowed my head and climbed again.

The lights and computer were off when I knocked on the door-frame to Roxana's office. She looked up from a manila file on her oak desk. "Hi, I'm Aaron," I said. Her office walls were papered with pictures of smiling Indian children and graduates and brides—all residents of BSSK before they were adopted. A white marker board hung crooked by the open window. Written on it was the number 4,105—the number of children the center had cared for since opening in 1979.

"Aah, Kirti-Ganga-Bhola's brother," Roxana said and let a pair of reading glasses slide down to the tip of her nose to look at me. A maroon shawl coolly draped her shoulders. The elastic waistband on my Calvin's was damp with sweat. "Sorry for the electricity. Every day we have eight-hour power outages from the drought."

"Oh, that's OK."

"You are looking warm."

"I'm getting used to the heat. Good thing you didn't see me last week."

After a few more minutes of conversation, she said, "Let us visit the children."

The most remarkable thing about the orphanage tour was how unremarkable it was. Every age group from newborns to first-graders had a play place stuffed with toys and a sleeping room lined with rows of cribs or bunk beds. More women in gold and green saris wandered each room, cradling and singing with the children, who fought and laughed with one another like family. The children ate daal (a lentil mixture) and chapatti (skinny pancakes) for lunch. If you were expecting Miss Hannigan to stumble drunk through a doorway or Mr. Bumble to be stingy on the gruel, you would not find them here.

The only noticeable difference between BSSK and any ordinary daycare was that it served as nightcare too. There was also play therapy for the older children and physical therapy for the disabled toddlers. The malnourished scabies-crawling tubercular-coughing children from my siblings' era were missing. They had been replaced by eighty healthy, happy children who backed up their soggy diapers into my lap to read a picture book or sing me the Indian national anthem.

As for the marker board's 4,105 other children in the BSSK family who no longer lived at the orphanage, they were sown around the globe. In the past few years, though, more and more Indian children had been adopted domestically. Today, BSSK's waiting list of Indian parents was longer than the list of children at BSSK awaiting families. That's a phenomenal change considering that fifteen years ago only one in five adoptions in India was domestic and now about four out of five Indian children are adopted in India.

Besides the noticeable rise of the Indian middle class, positive portrayals of adoption in the media were largely to thank for the transitioning ratio. There was also a growing open-mindedness in Indian culture that didn't exist in the '80s. When BSSK first opened its doors, Indian parents only wanted a male child or a fair-skinned child or a Hindu child. This cultural selectivity closed the door on the hope for thousands of orphans to ever be part of a loving family. International adoption reopened that door.

"Parenting is parenting," Roxana said when I asked what she thought about domestic versus international adoption. "We respect and appreciate all our adopting families and have wonderful and challenging experiences with both. Parenting is parenting whether or not it's by adoption. Or whether it's a family in India or Canada or Spain." Her reading glasses slumped to the tip of her nose.

I DROPPED MEREDITH THE FIRST WEEK she was home from India. She wriggled and I let go. At least I was the shortest kid in my first grade class so she didn't have very far to fall. But still. Meredith didn't cry when she collided with the kitchen linoleum. She pushed herself up using her fused fingers and laughed. She was a tough girl. I guess she had to be—that's how she had survived to her first birthday.

Every Friday in school we had show-and-tell when each student brought an item that was important to them to share with the class. Usually, kids would bring a round-faced Cabbage Patch doll or the New Kids On The Block pillow they slept with each night. I brought baby Meredith.

Mom and Dad waited in the hallway until it was my turn. As soon as my classmate Kevin had put his Donatello Ninja Turtle action figurine away, Mrs. Clark said, "Aaron, you can go get your show-and-tell now."

I poked my head out the doorway. "It's our turn," I squeaked. I also had the highest-pitched voice in my class—of all the boys and the girls.

"OK, now Aaron, can you tell the class who you brought for show-and-tell and why she's special to you?" Mrs. Clark said once my family was all inside the classroom and standing by the green chalkboard.

"This is my new sister. Her name's Meredith. She came home two weeks ago."

"How is she new?" another student asked. "Isn't she supposed to be more tiny? Like my new sister?"

"You're right, Jacob," Mom said. "She's not newborn but she's still new to our family. She was born almost a year ago in India."

"Is that why she's African American?"

"Well, she's not African American because she was born in India."

"So, so how did she get to here in Nebraska?"

"In the sky. On an airplane. Like a stork with a bigger engine."

"Will she know how to speak English or speak Indian?"

"Since we speak English I'm thinking she will too. Just like you and your parents speak English."

Meredith started to fidget in Mom's arms and she handed her over to Dad so she could play with his moustache.

"Can I pet her?"

"I don't think she likes being pet, Molly. But you can come introduce yourself and shake her hand."

Molly and a couple other girls dashed to the chalkboard to see.

"Hi Meredith, I'm Molly," she said taking Meredith's hand. "Uhm, what's wrong with her fingers?"

"I wanna see," one of the other girls said. "Eww! Weird."

Then the whole class dashed to the chalkboard.

"There's nothing wrong!" I said. "That's just how she came."

"How gross."

"It's not gross," Mom said. "What color hair were you born with?"

"Yellow."

"OK, well you were born with yellow hair and Meredith was born with fingers that go together. It's not gross. It's how it is."

"Yeah, but yellow hair is normal."

"She is normal," I said.

"All right." Mrs. Clark started scooting kids back to their desks. "Thank you, Aaron and Aaron's family for being such a conversation-starter today. Excellent show-and-tell."

"She is normal."

THE SCHOOL YEAR ENDED. The brown grass of winter that had turned green in spring was already waning toward brown again in the heat of the Nebraska summer. At night, thunder burst, but no raindrops pattered the roof. It was too hot for that. The city's water supply began to dry up in the drought, and the mayor enacted a rule that odd-numbered houses like ours on Marilynn Avenue could only water their lawns on odd-numbered days of the month. So on the first and third and fifth and so on of July, my parents turned on the sprinklers in the backyard for Meredith and me to run through. She crawled through them mainly. Or simply sat in the decaying grass in a swollen diaper waiting for the spigot to pivot in her direction. When it did, a rainbow-shaped waterfall splashed over her and she swatted at it with her hand wrapped in a plastic yellow sack from Piggly Wiggly Grocery. Underneath the sack was her first cast to encase and protect her newly severed fingers from infection.

In August the cast came off and the school year began anew. Mom and Dad dropped me off at my second grade classroom and Meredith at daycare before they both went to work. When we had developed a routine and our parents realized they could have more than one child without accidentally killing or forgetting about one of them, Mom's urges for more children returned.

"Aaron, how would you feel about having another brother or sister?" Dad asked one morning as the silver Buick pulled up to my school. "Another kid who'd be between you and Meredith's age you could play with."

"OK."

"Just OK?"

"Yeah. That's OK."

"The social worker says that there aren't many older kids who can be adopted at BSSK orphanage where we've applied. So this might not happen so I don't want you to get your hopes too high."

"OK."

"She also said there's a tiny chance there might be a brother and a sister or a sister and a sister who'd come to our home together. But like she said, that rarely ever happens."

"Totally OK, Dad."

"OK. Go be good."

I unlatched my seatbelt, swung my purple backpack over my left shoulder, and ran to the front door wearing my spandex bicycle shorts, unfazed by the most influential conversation of my life. I couldn't comprehend the future of my family any more than I could understand the future embarrassment I feel today when I see my old class photographs and I am the only kid in school who thought wearing shorts that revealed my underwear lines (and a little more) was totally OK.

It's no surprise what happened next. Two days later the social worker called and said, "There is an older brother and sister sibling set at BSSK with no family in India and they need yours." It was Ganga and Bhola—Michelle and Jordan. My parents said yes.

"The name Ganga's not going to work for a little girl on the prairie," Mom said after she hung up the phone. "We'll have to find something else to call her."

"How about Michelle?" Dad said.

"I once had a poodle named Michelle. So no."

"I really like Michelle."

"Like the Beatles song?"

"That one."

"Michelle Ganga Eske. Doesn't exactly have the nicest ring does it?"

"It's perfect."

Upon filing the adoption paperwork, Mom and Dad wrote a letter to their to-be children. It was dated 1991.

Dear Ganga and Bhola:

We are waiting to hear more about when you get to come home. We are very excited about your coming to America to join our family.

We are sending some new pictures of our family for you to look at. Also, we have sent you some fun stickers to play with and share with your friends if you wish.

It is now spring in Nebraska. In Nebraska it is very hot in the summer, although probably not as hot as it gets in Pune. However, in the winter it gets very, very cold here and snows a lot. We can get tired of the cold weather, and when spring comes with warm days, everyone gets very excited to play outside again.

School will be out for the summer the end of May. We can play and go to the zoo and parks this summer for fun. Plus we will put up a swimming pool in our backyard to splash in. It should be lots of fun. Then in September school will start for both of you but that will be fun too in a different way. We hope you will enjoy school as much as your brother and sister.

A few weeks ago a man and his wife came to visit you and took pictures of you for us. They live close to us and were taking your pictures so that we could have more beautiful pictures of you. They brought 4 children to America from BSSK. We certainly wished they could have brought you too.

We bought new beds for you to sleep in when you come home. Your bedrooms are almost ready. We just have to hang a big picture over Bhola's bed and clean his closet out and straighten out a closet for Ganga's toys and clothes. But really your rooms are ready for you to move in to now.

We think about you every day and wait for word of when you can come home. We love you!

Mommy and Daddy

During my week at BSSK, I got more than a visual of the place where my siblings used to sleep and wake up day after day. I started to get the feel of what it would have been like when they woke up all those days not knowing when they would have a family again. In the meantime, BSSK was home for them. And now for me. I shadowed the same nurses who had taught Michelle and Jordan to count and fed them rice and washed their backsides from soapy water in a bucket. But mostly, I played with the new generation of BSSK orphans. The kids were like cousins and the nurses like my great aunts to me—like the ones whose names I had read on captions in my grandmother's earlier black-and-white photo albums but whom I had never met because they were "still back there in the old country."

The greatest "aunt" of all was Mrs. Joshi, the now-retired director who opened BSSK in the 1970s and cared for three of my siblings. Her house was two blocks from the orphanage, and I visited her on my second day during naptime.

"Mrs. Joshi?" I hollered through the screen door, which was closed to shutter out the venomous mosquitoes buzzing around her garden.

"Ah, Aaron, come in please," she called back. "Please, come in."

I did and was greeted by a chubby golden lab with cloudy eyes. Mrs. Joshi's power was out, too, and the shadowy interior of her loft-style house was cast in a natural light from the long set of windows framing the banana trees in her backyard. The dog led me through the maze of haphazard furniture to the room where Mrs. Joshi sat erect in a lilac sari on a floral-print couch. Pictures of her family and of fighter planes were hanging on the walls at varying heights depending on her husband's mood when he hammered the nail in. Her wiry hair was pulled back in a bun. It was whiter than in the pictures Michelle and Jordan brought home of their going-away party.

"You'll have tea?" she asked, pouring me a cup. "And food? Lots of food for you, Aaron. You need to eat."

The tea steamed, and I took a spoonful of *namkeen,* a bird-seed-like spicy trail mix of dried chickpeas, watermelon seeds, lentil shreds, and raisins. We talked about BSSK, her husband, her friend and old co-worker Grandma Holt, and why I was there.

"So tell me about Ganga-Bhola," she said, repositioning the side of her sari, which had come loose. "I don't forget the older children. Ganga was very very motherly to Bhola . . . well, all the children. She would tell stories, made most of them up. But some were real."

"What were the stories about?"

"Heroes. She told heroic stories. And she would laugh. Does she still have her laugh?"

"Yeah but it came down a few octaves," I said. "Now she, Michelle—Ganga—is a nurse."

"A nurse. How old?"

"Twenty-four. Same age as me." Mrs. Joshi wobbled her head, disbelieving.

"And Bhola?"

"He's fine," I lied. "He joined the army." I didn't mention his early discharge or jail time.

"Is he happy?" she asked. I hesitated. She noticed. "I know Bhola will find his way. He was a good boy."

"Yeah, I hope so." I sipped the tea respectfully, burning my tongue as I did so.

"Do you know what Bhola means?"

Mortally confused came to mind, but I just said, "No."

"Naïve. Your brother's Indian name means naïve."

That would do. "You really don't forget the older children, do you," I said.

She used her arms as levers to stand from the cushy sofa, shuffled to the other side of the house, and rummaged through a drawer. "Come back tomorrow, Aaron. I have a thing to give Ganga-Bhola but cannot find it," she said once she had returned.

"Of course," I said and stood abruptly. "I'll see you tomorrow morning."

I retraced my steps to the screen door and emerged in the lush front garden. Once my eyes adjusted to the cloudy white concrete sky, they were lured to a purple flower rising two feet in the air out of a brick well.

"You like the blue lotus?" asked Mr. Joshi, who was gardening.

"Yes, it's beautiful." I said and walked nearer.

"It grows from deep in the mud, see? A seed in the mud."

"And it becomes this?" I pinched the healthy green stem.

"With good care."

"You and Mrs. Joshi have a very lovely garden, Sir."

The next morning I returned, and Mrs. Joshi greeted me at the door. "Ah, Aaron. Come in, please. Please, come in." She led me to the kitchen table upon which sat a freshly picked bunch of bananas the size of baby gorilla fingers and a used cardboard tea box wrapped in clear packing tape.

"I picked the fruit for you," she ordered. "I wrapped the box for Ganga-Bhola."

I unzipped my backpack and placed the box on the bottom where it would remain unopened for the next 12,000 miles. I cradled the dwarf bananas in my hand. "Thanks for everything," I said. "You know, you're a legend in my family."

Then, without warning, she hugged me. I didn't know how long it lasted or what we said once her body separated from mine. I didn't know if my knees bent to meet her low height or if she minded the yellow gorilla baby fingers poking her back. All I knew was the way it felt, its impossible effect on my nervous system. It was more scary than warm, more squishy than fuzzy. After weeks of being lonely in India, it felt like I was being hugged for the first time.

IN DEVELOPING COUNTRIES, CHILDREN ARE orphaned for three main reasons.

One: their parents have died and they have no other family to take care of them.

Two: their parents don't have the means to raise them.

Or, three: their parents can't raise them in the society they were born into.

The first scenario is pretty straightforward and most often occurs when diseases like cholera and AIDS or disasters like tsunamis and earthquakes kill children's parents. If the orphans have no living relatives and the authorities are alerted in time, they can be taken into custody and are generally placed in an orphanage or some form of community care.

The other two scenarios are a little more complicated. If this were a dictionary, an "orphan" would be a child without living parents. And if I were writing on behalf of an international organization, I would define an orphan as a child who has lost one or both parents. But these references do not fit the reality of millions of abandoned children with living parents, so I'm tossing out semantics and saying it like it is. The kid asleep on the cot in an orphanage whose teenage birth mother lives in the next village over has the same needs as every other orphan in the room. So, in this book when I say "orphan," I'm referring to any child who needs a family.

Impoverished parents, unable to feed one more mouth, lead the camp of moms and dads who voluntarily give up their children. They are joined by the parents who already have the maximum number of children their government allows, the parents who don't want a girl because girls mean marriage dowries and lower pay for the jobs they do, and the parents who can't pay for the medical treatment of a child born with severe special needs like cerebral palsy or blindness. Those are some reasons children in developing countries are orphaned.

The last group of orphans are those conceived in socially unacceptable circumstances. These are the children of an unmarried fifteen-year-old Hindu mother whose unwed pregnancy will stain her life. The children of rape victims. The children of a mixed-race or mixed-caste love affair never meant to leave the sheets. Essentially, these children are the crying proof of a taboo sexual act, a taboo that is upheld at all costs, even the life of the child.

Not all infants whose parents cannot keep them are abandoned on railway station platforms or in marketplaces or temples. Those who are, are typically found in pretty bad shape—sunburned, hungry, dehydrated, rat-bitten. An encouraging number of parents are choosing to relinquish their babies directly to orphanages, hoping they will be loved by a family that can.

UNICEF, the United Nations branch in charge of the rights of children, estimates that 132 million children in the world meet their definition of "orphan." Seventy-two million in Asia. Forty-six million in sub-Saharan Africa. To put these numbers in perspective, there are about 80 million children in total in the United States. So if every child in the United States were an "orphan," every Boy Scout and flower girl you see, then there would still be 52 million orphans left over. That's how many orphans there are in our world. That's the severity. That's the need.

The caveat you have to remember though is that UNICEF's estimate of the number of orphans worldwide is imperfect. It includes kids whose dads have died and who are still living with their moms like Michelle and Jordan did before their mom eventually died as well. And the UNICEF figure does not include kids like Meredith, whose parents are still alive but are unable to care for their children. No one knows exactly how large the number of real orphans is. We only know it's enormous.

The international community recognized the enormity of the global orphan crisis in the 1993 Hague Convention on Protection of Children and Co-operation. The landmark multilateral treaty spells out the law for international adoption and was ratified by the United States in 2007. The document is thick in legalese, but its point is simple: it is better for a child to be adopted by an international family than it is for the child to spend his or her life in a domestic orphanage. The goal is always to keep a child in a family in his or her home country, but when that isn't feasible, then a home in another country is better than none.

I ALSO WELCOMED MY NEW family members in a letter.

Dear Ganga and Bhola:

I am your new brother. I am seven years old and I go to school at Beattie School. We do lots of things like play games and read books. We get to school in a car.

We have a young baby from BSSK. We have a mom and dad who will never leave you.

Bhola will go to school at Trinity. Ganga will go to school at Beattie. Your new names will be American names, but we haven't decided what they are yet.

Your grandmother and grandfather are very nice. Grandfather is very funny. Grandmother is very nice. They live in the same town. They are very kind.

Love,

Your Brother

Aaron

Chapter Six

REINCARNATIONS

One morning in May 1991, Michelle and Jordan put the drawings they had kept in the orphanage and two changes of clothes in a sack. That night they were boarding their first airplane ever, pointed at the United States. Before they left, BSSK gave them a farewell party.

Ten older children were lined in two rows of five in the crowded orphanage nursery room. Boy-girl-boy-girl. Nine pairs of arms hula-waved to the right, but one absent-minded pair waved to the left. A mid-tempo Bollywood tune played on the stereo donated by a family in Texas. The lines transformed into a handholding circle, and the twenty bare feet moved in and out like a fish's mouth. When they weren't concentrating too hard on their next gesture, the children remembered to smile for the audience of nurses, staff, and squirming infants. Michelle and Jordan sat in the front row, watching their friends dance them good-bye. The steps were the same as every other farewell ceremony the two had performed in for the past years while they waited for it to be their turn.

A girl whose shaved hair had grown into a bowl cut the same length as Michelle's left the dancers and walked toward Michelle and Jordan. She grabbed their hands and pulled them into the troupe for the dance's last stanza. They waved their arms to the rhythm with their friends. The music ended, and the children encircled Michelle and Jordan in a good-bye hug. Standing tall in the audience, Mrs. Joshi admired her garden.

IN INDIA'S ANCIENT VARANASI, NASA-Jeff and I did not speak on the dinghy. What do you say when you're rowing along the holiest mile of the holiest river in the world?

The Ganga River, or the Ganges in colonial English, stretches 1,560 miles from the Himalayas to the Bay of Bengal. On the way it passes Varanasi, a city Mark Twain described as "older than history, older than tradition, older even than legend, and looks twice as old as all of them put together." Around the time David was slinging Goliath, King Tut was a teenage pharaoh, Troy was tricked by a horse, and Romulus was naming Rome, Hindus were bathing in Varanasi's sacred waters. Three thousand years later, a million pilgrims voyage to the city's storied riverbank each year. I was one.

Legend has it that the Ganga River is the earthly form of the goddess Ganga, who slid down a lock of Shiva's hair to bless the physical world with Brahman—the transcendental origin and final destination of all the time, energy, space, matter, feeling, life, and death in our universe. If you could hear Brahman, it would probably sound like the security line at Chicago's O'Hare Airport on Christmas Eve. If you could touch it, I imagine it would feel like the inside of a lion's mouth. If you could see it, it would without a doubt look like Varanasi at 8:00 PM on a Wednesday.

The Ganga's current was the color of chai tea, like chocolate milk with a swirl of tar. The river breeze smelled sulfuric like the

Fourth of July—minus the burgers. The only sounds were the chanting of ghat bathers and the creaking of wooden oars as they pulled the boat and its passengers through the sludgy water. In addition to NASA-Jeff and me on the boat, one man and one boy rowed at the helm. The older and fatter was an Indian John Belushi look-alike with chipped red teeth. The younger looked nervous and wrenched his oar like a robot in need of oil. A much older man along for the ride sat cross-legged in the bed of the boat like a bespectacled Mahatma Gandhi. The hair on his head was white, but the three inches of fuzz rising vertically out of his ears were coal black. No one broke the silent enchantment.

On shore, the ancient pastel buildings of Varanasi reflected in thc Ganga below. Hundreds of Hindus gathered on the stepped ghats. The men wore sarongs tied with string at their navels and the women were a fluttering rainbow of saris. The worshipers descended step by step into the obscure water until only the black tips of their floating hair were visible. Then, with open eyes they sprang up and down in the river, spitting out mouthfuls of water at each jump's crest. The locals performed this ritual repeatedly each day. Others traveled weeks for the chance.

Many pilgrims voyaged to Varanasi not to worship, but to die. A row of mummified corpses wrapped in white rested on the Manikarnika Ghat. They were patiently waiting their turn to be thrown on the bonfire. Those who could afford it paid for their bodies to be cremated and sown across the Ganga. The bodies of those who could not pay were laid whole in the river and sunk with a rock placed on their chest beside the thousands of others. By returning their souls to the holy Varanasi waters, Hindus believed they would attain *moksha,* or salvation, and escape reincarnation's infinity of life and death and life and death.

Corpses weren't the only things lurking in the Ganga. Because Varanasi's medieval sewage system trickles down the ghats and into the river, the fecal bacteria count of the Ganga is 4,000 times the World Health Organization's bathing standard limit. A billion liters of raw sewage flows into the Ganga every day, infecting its bathers with typhoid, polio, and dysentery. Yet despite its risks, devout Hindus plunge into the river day after decaying day without hesitation, so assured are they of its cleansing powers.

The best view of this ritual was from the water. The sky and river were hazy navy as the man and boy turned the dinghy around to row us home for the night. Halfway there, a field of lotus-shaped votive candles drifted toward us in the river. The rowing ceased, and without the oars' guidance we spun in place. Whichever direction the boat carouseled, my head pivoted to behold the votives, glittering gold in the twilight. The flames ushered the ashes of the dead who rode their universe one last time while the living washed themselves in its life.

PEOPLE'S HEARTS TICK IN WAYS that inspire them to do crazier things than swim in cesspools with incinerated bodies. Teenagers in Peru join a monastery and vow a life of celibacy. Ten mountain climbers in Nepal go up Mount Everest knowing that, statistically, only nine will come down. And a white middle-class couple in Nebraska say yes to adopting two older orphans from the opposite side of the earth when all they know about them are their names.

We traveled to pick up Michelle and Jordan, but not all the way to India—only to the Minneapolis airport. Following the recent assassination of India's Prime Minister Rajiv Gandhi, it had been deemed unsafe for foreigners to fly to India.

"Here they come," Mom said when she spotted them walking along the maroon carpet of the breezeway connecting the airplane to the airport. She put her hand atop Dad's.

Dad took a small and sleeping Jordan in his arms from the woman who had escorted him and Michelle to the United States.

Mom ran over to Michelle, who flinched at the tall blond woman and stepped backward.

"Hi Ganga . . . Hi Michelle."

Michelle froze. A white plastic bag she held with both hands swayed in front of her. It was nearly empty but contained everything she owned in the world. Bangle bracelets stacked up her arms.

"This is Aaron, your brother."

A slight smile.

"And that's Daddy."

Michelle's eyes flashed back to me. We looked at each other in mutual wonder. She at my pale skin, neon '90s shorts, and bowl cut. I at her pocked skin, blue sari, and bowl cut. On her feet was a pair of mismatched tennis shoes. The big toe of the darker shoe looked as if an animal had taken a bite out of it but really it had just been sliced open so it didn't rub against the place where her big toenail would have been had it not fallen off the week before from an infection.

Standing there in the airport terminal, it was not brotherhood at first sight. We still felt like the foreigners we really were. Mom and Dad's parental instincts kicked in from the moment Michelle and Jordan landed, but I didn't have that kind of obligation. I was just a child meeting another child who had grown up in a different country, spoke a different language, played different games, feared different horrors, and got around differently, on an elephant for all I knew. The only thing we had in common was our parents.

Michelle reached in her sack and pulled out a photo album tied with string. Pictures of her friends at the orphanage were pasted to its yellowing pages. The last photo was of us, her new family. We had mailed it to India along with our letters so Michelle and Jordan would know the strangers they were going to be starting their new lives with.

Mom took Michelle's left hand and pointed at the bag in her right. "Can I carry? Can Aaron carry?"

Michelle carried her bag.

ON OUR FIRST NIGHT ALL TOGETHER in Nebraska, Michelle and Jordan slept on the fuzzy blue rug in Meredith's nursery. This sleeping arrangement actually lasted for about the first month after their arrival. They had their own rooms but slept better in a cluster as they always had. They still liked having their own toys, own closet, own clothes. Just not their own beds. I liked mine just fine and slept alone every night.

When Jordan had night terrors and woke up wailing and kicking so hard he couldn't stop himself, Michelle walked across the hall to Mom and Dad's bedroom. She tiptoed over to Mom's side of the bed and stood there, barely taller than the mattress, and whispered, "Mom . . . Mom . . . Mom . . . Jordan crying." Since the moment she had stepped off the airplane, Michelle had abdicated her role as Jordan's mother. Mom had expected to have to plan a coup d'état to wrestle Michelle for the right but after all those years as his guardian, Michelle had had enough and handed over the keys to Jordan's new family.

So Mom got out of bed and put a bathrobe over the knee-length T-shirt she slept in and followed Jordan's cries. She scooped him off the ground and carried him into the hallway where she sat and rocked him up and down.

"I know this must be scary for you, Bhola. But you're OK," she told him even though he probably didn't understand. I heard her outside my closed bedroom door but did not bother to go out and help. I was still adjusting, too.

He whimpered back some words in Marathi that she definitely didn't understand.

"You're OK," she said over and over again until his fear and anger melted away and he fell back to sleep.

Michelle was not about to give up control of her own sovereignty as easily as she did Jordan's.

"It's dinnertime, Michelle!" Mom called from the slit in the wall between the kitchen and the living room where Michelle was crouched on the floor watching *I Love Lucy*. She really did love Lucy. Not only was Lucille Ball Michelle's favorite source of laughter, she also taught her how to speak English. Michelle would watch two episodes every night, and before she knew what word to call a refrigerator she'd already learned the difference between a ragtop and a wet rag.

"Not yet, Mom!" Michelle called back.

"Now Michelle!"

"But Ethel cutting Lucy spaghetti with scissors."

"Come on, Michelle. No more TV."

Then the screaming began. "No no NO!" She rolled on the floor, pounded her fists, and shook her short hair.

"Stop that, Michelle!" Mom ran into the room.

"No. No. No. No. No."

"It's just time for dinner. And it's just a TV show."

"No tell me what to do."

"I will. I'm your mother. That's what I'm here for."

"No my mother! No have mother. Hate my mother. No need mother."

"I think you do."

"No." Michelle flailed her body on the ground again.

"You're not going to scare me away, Michelle. You can try but it's not going to work. I know a lot of people have left you alone in the world and you were very good at taking care of yourself."

"You going to leave me too!"

"I will never leave you and Jordan."

"Yes."

"No, Dad and I will never leave you. Always love you."

"No."

"Never leave you."

Michelle relented and came to dinner, but this fight turned into a recurring theme of the season. She and Mom would have to repeat this episode five or six more times before Michelle could finally believe that she was not just one commercial break away from abandonment.

MEREDITH TURNED TWO YEARS OLD in July, and we celebrated with a picnic table dinner in the backyard. It wasn't all that different from every other dinner of the first summer. If it wasn't raining, we always ate outside so when we were finished us kids could go play in the grass while Dad got out the gardening hose and power washed the table and the chairs and the ground to clean away the mashed potatoes and chicken bones that had been dropped or thrown during the meal.

My parents invited Prakash, an Indian-American computer programmer who spoke Hindi and Marathi, to Meredith's birthday party, and he was brave enough to accept.

"Namasté, Michelle," Prakash said when she answered the door.

"Hello."

"Ap kaisi hai?"

"What?"

"You don't remember Hindi?"

"No. I am in America."

"Oh, I see."

Michelle ran out to the backyard to practice her cartwheels in a pink dress. She didn't wear pants once that summer. Or that winter even. She had never had a closet full of her own outfits before and now that she did, she wanted a dress on every hanger.

"Namasté, Jordan."

"Kya chal raha hai," Jordan said.

"Accha."

"Hi Prakash," Dad said.

"Hi there, Jim."

"The pizza's on its way. I've also been experimenting with some chicken tikka and Deb's making naan."

"Sounds great."

"You're welcome to come work in the kitchen with us or out back with the kids if you want to have more fun."

"I'll go out back, thanks."

A few minutes later Prakash reappeared in the kitchen. Dad was standing over a simmering orange pan. I was loitering beside him, wanting to be on my parents' side of the grown-up/child divide. I spent plenty of time playing with my siblings too, but sometimes I attached myself to my parents—an only child again if only for a few minutes.

"Jim, Jordan wants to know where your toolkit is."

"Oh, for the tricycle?"

"Yeah. Well it's more like a bicycle now that the front wheel's fallen off."

"He broke that this morning," I tattled. "Wasn't watching where he was going and drove it full-speed into the house."

"The trike looks pretty hopeless doesn't it. I scoped it out earlier and think it's a goner," Dad said.

"He swears he can fix it."

"OK, Aaron will you go get the toolkit from the garage?"

"He's not going to fix it. He doesn't know how." I said, not wanting Jordan interrupting any of my time alone with my parents.

"You're probably right but let's let him try, OK?"

Ten minutes later I went outside to put pizza boxes on the picnic table. Jordan was sitting on the repaired tricycle pedaling with his small legs as fast as he could through the grass.

After two months of dining practice in the backyard, our parents thought we were ready for a nighttime family outing. So they chose to go to the most public place in Lincoln—Friday night dinner at the shopping mall food court. I didn't know who was being braver—my parents for taking the chance on a social disaster or my new brother and sister for daring to make their debut in a scary new world. The outcome of all this courage has become not only a family legend, but Lincoln folklore. It may seem silly, but eating that night at the food court was a pivotal step for us, like graduating from bottles to solid foods.

"OK, everybody sit," Mom said. "Michelle, you here."

Michelle gazed into the Disney Store.

"Michelle sit down. Please sit here Michelle. OK . . . or you can sit there."

Michelle was beside Meredith, buckling her into her booster seat.

"Aaron, stay here with everybody while Dad and I get food. What does everybody want from Mr. Panda?"

"Cashew chicken."

"Egg rolls."

"I rove flied lice," Jordan said.

It took Jordan four years to learn how to pronounce American *r*s and *th*s and talk like a local.

"Onetwothreefour," Mom counted her kids when she and Dad returned with four trays of Chinese food.

"Good, haven't lost anybody yet," Dad said.

Midway through his "flied lice" Jordan said, "I have to baffroom."

Mom pointed him to the gray door with a stick man on it and he walked alone. Ten minutes passed, and the little guy still hadn't returned.

"Aaron, go check on your brother."

I went in after him. Behind the gray door I saw Jordan's small stonewashed jeans on the floor. He was half-naked and sitting on the rim of the urinal. His legs dangled. A man washed his hands, pretending not to notice. Jordan wasn't finished.

"Hi Air-win."

I exited the bathroom. "He's pooping in the urinal!" I screamed to the whole food court. I'm not sure why. It just felt right to let everyone know what bizarre sideshow act was happening in the restroom while they ate their dinner.

"What?" I heard Mom yell back over the other tables.

"He's pooping! In the urinal!"

"Well go get him down!"

Back in the bathroom, he was still going. The bowl was nearly full.

"Jordan, that's not a toilet."

"Hi Air-win."

"Come on, get off."

"I'm not done!"

"Jordan, get off!" I took his hand, which had been holding onto the flush lever for balance. I tugged. He tugged back.

"Not done!"

"You have to be done. You're running out of room."

I tugged again. He kicked with his naked leg.

"Fine. Finish."

He did. Hopped down. Put his pants back on. Looked pleased with his first successful use of a public restroom. He didn't understand he had done it all wrong.

Mom took maternity leave for the whole summer to devote extra time to raising her new children. Every single day in June, July, and August we walked to Shopko—a superstore full of Americana four blocks from our house. And every night when she went to bed, Mom would thank God for once again giving her the strength not to kill one of her children on the way.

Before we started our walks, Mom would line us up in a row by the door and remind us of the rules.

"What do we not do?" she'd ask us.

"No hitting."

"No biting."

"No kicking."

"No wandering."

"You're still missing one."

"No peeing in corners."

I pushed a two-year-old Meredith in the stroller while Mom minded Jordan and Michelle's every move. Jordan hated walking and sat his four-year-old butt on the pavement at every intersection and refused to move. Usually, Mom would take him by the wrist and pull him to the other side of the street like a wagon without wheels. Michelle had the opposite problem and wandered into busy streets as if she still lived in India and was begging among traffic. Whenever she was about to be run over by a car, Mom would yell, "Ganga Bus! Ganga Bus!" at her. I'm sure our neighbors wondered why Mom didn't know the difference between a bus and a car, but what they didn't know is that "Bus!" means "Stop!" in Marathi and it was *the* word of the summer of '91.

"Bus!" she'd yell if Jordan was climbing on the roof of the Buick. "Bus!" she screamed when Michelle got out the scissors to cut Meredith's hair. "Bus bus bus!" was typically the only word spoken when we went to the candy store with the giant bins of gobstoppers and chocolate bon-bons that Michelle and Jordan treated like their own personal trick-or-treating sacks as they reached right in.

When we finally arrived at Shopko, we would walk the aisles learning new vocabulary like "soap," "marker," and "don't touch the china." One day after being caught eating a bag of M&Ms he had grabbed off the shelf, Jordan plopped down in the middle of the greeting cards aisle and refused to move. At the same time, Meredith began throwing a tantrum to wriggle loose from her stroller, Michelle started wandering away, and I was running between the three of them like a rodeo clown.

"Buuuss!" Mom boomed.

A nearby woman put down the Cathy comic strip birthday card she was reading, walked over and said, "Welfare mother, eh? I bet each of these children has a different father, too."

"Yes, you're very observant, Madam." Mom deepened her voice like she does so well when she's about to spank you with words. Having experienced this force, we all could sense she was about to burst and froze in well-behaved anticipation. "Each of my children does have a different biological father because they're adopted. And I suppose you could say I'm a welfare mom, but only because I am the director of the Department of Social Services."

Mom never did respond kindly to unfair criticism. It's a trait I guess I've inherited. Before I began my round-the-world exploration, I was strolling through the British Museum with a friend who said, "Look at all these amazing things that were taken from other countries to be here in this museum. Don't hate me for saying this, but isn't taking a child from his home country kind of the modern-day equivalent to removing a statue from the Parthenon?"

I didn't know what to say. Now I do.

The concern does have the weight of history behind it since there's an ugly precedent of "do-gooders" invading other countries in the name of preservation, God, and the future of humanity.

The modern-day humanitarians without borders craze started in 1863 when Henry Dunant created the world's first international humanitarian organization, the International Red Cross, for which he was awarded the first Nobel Peace Prize. He founded the organization after witnessing the need for wounded soldiers to be neutrally cared for when wounded in battle.

By 1909, 176 international humanitarian organizations in the world had followed Dunant's model. That number catapulted to at least 23,135 by 1996. There's now a $60 billion a year industry dedicated to doing "good" in the world—treating cholera in Peru, arguing for human rights in China, teaching girls math in Afghanistan. But sometimes the people behind these well-intentioned projects have been drinking the Ganges, and their goodwill goes bad. No cause is immune—especially not international adoption.

Looking back at history, it is not a coincidence that on a timeline of the nineteenth century, the global spread of Christian-based humanitarianism aligns with the global spread of colonialism. One of the era's most notorious colonialists, Cecil Rhodes (the man after whom the Rhodes Scholarship and once-upon-a-time Rhodesia were named) summarized the twisted overlap best when he announced "colonialism is philanthropy plus five percent."

Mr. Rhodes would not fare well in today's political discourse where imperialism is about as fashionable as a whalebone corset. The classic empire is dead. The concept isn't gone, though. It has merely been given a flashy new feel-good name: humanitarianism. Rich nations used to be able to enter a foreign land and poach the natives until they were so beaten they would let you rename their country after yourself. Now we enter countries through conditional food aid and armed peace soldiers—in the name of humanitarianism, of course.

So how does this ethical trapdoor affect international adoption agencies? Children are precious resources and, like any resource, they are sometimes used and exploited. In Cambodia and Guatemala, corrupt adoption agencies and lawyers paid mothers a few hundred dollars in exchange for newborn children. These agencies and lawyers would then mark up the child's resale value to the six-figure range and sell him or her to unaware families in the United States. There are also reports of Guatemalan children who had been kidnapped reappearing later in U.S. homes. Once U.S. authorities were alerted to this abuse, they froze all pending adoptions from the country until the Guatemalan government could guarantee the children it was sending to U.S. families were being given voluntarily and not sold or stolen.

Then there are the cases of child smuggling motivated by something more dangerous than profit: piety. The zealous beliefs that God or goodness ordains something, and that therefore it must be carried out, exist in many aspects of a believer's life. Most liquor stores in America are closed on Sundays. Some women shroud every inch of their bodies except their eyelids in black cloaks even during the middle of summer. Other believers refuse to cut their steak with the same knife they used to cut a block of cheddar cheese.

In 2007, six members of the Paris-based organization Zoe's Ark embarked on a mission to airlift 103 children out of Darfur. These humanitarians claimed the children were Sudanese orphans, and they planned to care for them in France. In fact, the children were from nearby Chad, and many still had at least one living parent and were not eligible for adoption. No matter how good their intentions were, the members of Zoe's Ark overstepped legal and ethical bounds. Too pious for their own good, they were sentenced to eight years of forced labor. Eventually, they were pardoned by the government of Chad in March 2008, after spending nearly a year in a French prison.

After the global media demonized Zoe's Ark, it didn't seem likely that another group would make the same mistake soon. But humanitarianism sometimes suffers from short-term memory loss. On January 12, 2010, a 7.0-magnitude earthquake devastated Port-au-Prince, the capital city of Haiti. Buildings collapsed, hospitals, roads, airports, and phone lines were destroyed. Hundreds of thousands of people died, making many new orphans in a small country that already had tens of thousands. An improvised group of ten Baptists from Idaho, the New Life Children's Refuge, sprang into action and flew to Haiti, convinced that they knew how to help the children on an impoverished island that most of them had never traveled to before. They believed that the work would not require experience because they were on a mission from God.

The official mission of the New Life Children's Refuge was to care for "orphaned, abandoned and impoverished Haitian and Dominican children, demonstrating God's love and helping each child find healing, hope, joy and new life in Christ." News channels around the world reported that when they arrived in Haiti, they rounded up thirty-three Haitian children without documentation, but mostly with parents. Then the Americans started driving the Haitian children on a bus into the Dominican Republic on the other half of the island. The missionaries were stopped at the border, where they could not provide any paperwork or authorization to take the children out of Haiti. They were arrested and placed in a Haitian jail, which was newly empty since all the former prisoners had escaped in the earthquake's aftershock.

In the 1950s, the Holts were inspired by a 2,000-year-old passage in the Bible to pioneer international adoption. However, my parents' faith was not what motivated them to adopt. We went to church each Sunday but only because it was part of our rituals, like our forced marches to Shopko. Mom and Dad's core belief was that a good day was a fully scheduled day.

So on Sunday mornings we would put on our dresses and clip-on bowties and go to First Plymouth Church. Mom and Dad chose it above all the other churches in Lincoln because the sermons weren't too preachy and the music was the best in town. It also had a balcony where we could sit by ourselves during the service in case Meredith or Jordan had a fit, or Michelle started asking questions loudly.

"Who is that dead man hanging on the tree?"

"What do the candles mean?"

"When you go to heaven is that like being reborn on Earth?"

When church was over and the bell tower chimed Bach, we squeezed into Dad's Buick and drove to the Village Inn diner for Sunday brunch. Mom and Dad ordered us pancakes with blueberry eyes and bacon smiles. Everyone in the restaurant stared at us, probably thinking "those parents are cuckoo," and maybe they were right. Mom and Dad didn't see it that way. Like the bathers in the filthy Ganga River, they didn't feel insane, they felt love and devotion for something they knew was right.

That's the difference between an artifact and an orphan retrieved from faraway countries—love. One is treasure in a glass case and the other is treasured in a home.

The foundation for faith-based humanitarian organizations and adoption agencies can be far-fetched to the point of crazy and dangerous, but despite the menacing asterisks in the mix, you have to hand it to them for trying. Even though missionaries sometimes have ulterior motives and righteous attitudes, it's not nice to imagine the world without the work of worthy organizations.

If all forms of goodwill can be flawed, one might argue that we should let the local populations sort out their troubles on their own.

We could end humanitarian interventions and international adoptions entirely and cross our fingers that it will work. But that's a lot like yelling "Breathe!" to a choking person. Rwandan genocide victims were not twiddling their thumbs as they were hacked to death with machetes. They simply didn't have the means to solve the problem on their own at the time. The same is true about most countries with too many orphans and too few resources to care for them in loving family settings. These countries and children need a lifesaver, and that is where the responsible Hague-abiding international adoption agencies and big-hearted wannabe parents intervene. It's not a flawless solution. We must be vigilant to ensure that safeguards are put in place so that corrupt baby-selling lawyers in Cambodia and misguided organizations like Zoe's Ark in North Africa and New Life Children's Refuge in Haiti don't get away with their criminal activity. But for now, once all the safety boxes are checked, international adoption is giving millions of children a new chance at life.

Chapter Seven

"All the Best"

"HOWDY, ESKES," THE NURSE GREETED US in the white tiled hospital hallway. Three months earlier, we'd had no idea who she was. But we'd been around for her shift so many times that we had learned how many spreads of peanut butter she liked on her sandwiches.

"Hello Sharon!" Mom called back, recognizing from a distance the woman's bushy bangs hairsprayed stiff.

"Who's getting the knife today?"

"It's Meredith's turn."

"But she's still got her cast from last time on her leg."

"Yeah. Today we're operating on the other one."

Meredith smiled proudly.

"I'll tell ya. You guys are the most famous family of the summer around this place. Even more than that man who staple-gunned his belly button shut."

"We try, right, kids? Eight surgeries in three months is pretty good. At least we're getting our money's worth out of our health insurance plan this year."

"I'll say. How many more operations y'all got?"

"This is it. I think."

"We hope," Dad added.

"I'll say. Will you be back in to take out Jordan's stitches?"

"I'll just yank them out at home. That's elementary for us now—like Band-Aids."

"Well, we'll miss havin' you around. Hospital's almost your home!"

There was no almost about it. I spent more hours that summer in the surgical waiting room of St. Elizabeth's Hospital than I did outside. We were there so often we had started to just leave our toys in the magazine rack overnight because we knew we'd be back for them soon enough.

Meredith's surgeries on her warped feet and legs had been in the works for years. The first orthopedic surgeon to examine her foot when she came home told Mom and Dad, "If we amputate her foot now then we'll be able to fit her for a prosthesis before she learns to walk. It's easier that way."

"You want to saw off our daughter's foot?"

"Yes. Or she will never walk."

"I don't believe it."

"I'm sorry. I know that's not easy to hear. But that's the best we can do for her medically."

"Doctor, this girl used to weigh three pounds and grew up on a metal tray in a shanty hospital. Now look at her. She's been defying medical books her whole life and I won't deny her the chance to do it again."

"She can't . . ."

"Like Jim said, we don't believe it."

"But . . ."

"In 16 years, she'll be dancing on her own two feet at prom." Mom said and they left his office.

The next surgeon inspected every angle of Meredith's C-shaped foot for ten minutes before he spoke. "This is a good foot. We can do a lot with it. In a few years when she's old enough we'll probably have to rearrange the bones in there. But you know, this is a good foot."

Jordan's surgeries that summer weren't so preordained. When he first arrived from India, two foreign infections plagued his body. Even though they were unrelated, both infections produced the same nuclear green color—one pussed from sores on Jordan's palms and the other oozed down his upper-lip from his nose.

The green hand sores were the result of scabies parasites that had burrowed under his skin. They itched so much Jordan had scratched the bumps wide open and they became infected in the Indian elements. As soon as he got to America, the doctors gave Jordan an ointment to heal the sores and told Mom and Dad to buy a tub of insecticide for the rest of the family. The scabies had already spread through our house and were busy reproducing under the skin of our knee pits and elbows.

The doctors weren't so quick to cure the green gobs of slime that dripped from Jordan's nose in dollops. If the snot were honey, Jordan could have produced enough to marinate a dozen honey-baked hams a day. Mom's remedy was to get Jordan to blow his nose.

"OK, I'm holding the Kleenex, Jordan. Now blow!"

"Pbhwh," his lips puttered.

"With your nose, Jordan. Not your mouth."

"Pbbwhwh!"

"OK, I guess I'll just wipe your nose until the doctors figure out what to do."

Mom was still wiping more than a year later. None of the doctors—ear, nose, and throat specialists or infectious disease experts—knew how to stop the green. They irrigated his sinuses, which turned out to be doctor speak for giving his nostrils a power carwash. The green went away for a week after that but only because it was replaced with the hot red of a perpetually bloody nose. Then the green returned.

"Dr. Roth, there must be a way," Mom said at our spring family check-up. "What else is there?"

"There are two ways actually but they both suck."

"OK. Give 'em to me."

"There's only one prescription medicine that will cure Jordan's infection. But it will also stop him from growing for the rest of his life."

"Being three feet tall forever isn't a very good option. What else have you got?"

"The only other alternative is to surgically install a catheter into his heart and pump meds directly into his bloodstream exactly every three hours every day for the next three months."

"I can do it," Mom said and grabbed her calendar from her purse to find a spare day for surgery. "I have to save the kid."

"I don't recommend it, Deb."

"Do we have any other options?"

"No. But you can't . . ."

"Dave, tell me . . . if it was your daughter, what would you do?"

"Make sure every day every three hours for three months I was there to inject drugs into her catheter."

"Thought so. When can I start on my son?"

The morning after Jordan's last day of kindergarten, Dr. Roth attached a catheter to his heart that dangled from his chest like a limp dart pinned to a dartboard. Twice a week the hospital courier delivered frozen IV bags of medicine to our house. And every three hours, every day and every night, Mom was there to give Jordan his injection. All the while, Jordan's nose leaked green or red fluid.

Mom continued the treatment for two months until one night she went to his bedside and he was sweating.

"Are you OK, Jordan?"

She opened his eyelids, but he couldn't focus his pupils on hers. She got the thermometer.

"106. Shit."

Mom disconnected the IV, stripped Jordan, and hustled him to the bathroom, where she cranked the cold faucet on high.

"Jim—ice cubes," she said when Dad appeared in the doorway.

"What?"

"He's 106. His brains are gonna burn."

"Shit."

"He's allergic to the drugs. They're making him sick."

Dad returned with a plastic bag of ice from the fridge, tore it open and poured the ice cubes into the tub where Jordan lay comatose like a straw in a giant vodka on the rocks. Mom kept the back of her hand to his forehead, waiting for the temperature to drop. Her nightgown was soaked with ice water and her own anxious sweat.

Thirty minutes later Jordan's fever broke. He shivered as Mom toweled him off. Dad grabbed a second towel and started drying off his back as Mom finished his legs.

"So what now?" Dad asked.

"We find a new way to save him."

Mom and Dad scheduled Jordan's surgery to remove the tubes from his chest on the same day that Meredith was scheduled to have the second phase of her foot operation.

"Killing two birds with one stone," Mom told us, as if she'd just made an appointment for them to get side-by-side haircuts.

The hospital staff assigned Meredith and Jordan to the same recovery room so we could wait for them to shake off their anesthesia together. Michelle and I shared an electric reclining chair in the corner, lowering and raising it until the motor got tired and the chair got stuck fully stretched back.

"Who do you think will wake up first?" I asked Michelle, lying there, elbows touching and looking up at the fluorescent light in the ceiling.

"Meredith."

"I say Jordan. Wanna bet a Snickers bar from the vending machine?"

"Yeah. Pinky swear?"

She held out her hand with her pinky extended. I looped mine around hers.

"Pinky swear."

Dr. Roth knocked on the door. "I've got good news, guys," I heard him say, still looking up at the water-stained tiles in the ceiling.

"You have a prescription for Valium in your pocket with my name on it?" Mom guessed.

"Better. I was talking to a buddy of mine up at Mayo about Jordan's sinuses. He has a crazy idea."

"Good. We're good at crazy."

"He thinks Jordan's immune system was fighting this infection for so long in India that it's stuck on autopilot and has kept fighting it even though we killed the bug months ago."

"So then all we have to do is give his immune system a chill pill."

"That's not exactly the technical term for it, Deb. But yes—a $3.70 dose of Prednisone may be all he needs to stop the green."

The dose was all he needed. And it wouldn't have been possible had he stayed in India. Michelle couldn't have won her battle against tuberculosis either if a doctor hadn't handed her a $10 bottle of pills. It was the same $10 bottle of pills that could have cured her ailing mother and changed the course of our lives. Michelle and Jordan's birth mother would have lived. They would not have moved to a new home in America with two new siblings. We would not have argued about who got to ride in the front seat of the Buick between Mom and Dad on our drives to the hospital that summer. Meredith would not have sleep-kicked Michelle in the face with her cast while they shared a bed. And then Michelle would not have had a black eye that looked a little like the shape of Texas.

I would not have had an undying case of Indian parasitic head lice and an idiot's haircut as a result. Every hairstylist in town refused to cut it except one, who at first failed to notice that my hair crept at the roots. When she did notice, she set the scissors down, refusing to finish.

And Mom would not have had such a large family standing over her asking how bad her body hurt on the night at the pizza buffet when she slipped on a loose ravioli on the floor and broke her leg. We had gone out to celebrate Jordan's sinuses.

We had all that, we had our family, because of a $10 bill. Ten dollars that Michelle and Jordan's mom did not have before she died.

"Howdy, Eskes!"

"Hi Sharon. We're back."

"I see that. I thought you were supposed to be all done."

"We were. And then I fell." Mom tapped her crutches on the hospital tile. "I'm here for a check-up."

"Oh my word! I didn't even notice *yours,* Deb. Too busy checking out the rest of 'em." Sharon's eyeballs zigzagged from the casts on both of Meredith's legs to the crusty brown blood in Jordan's nostrils to the purple bruise on Michelle's eye and then upward to my halfway haircut. Mom and Dad begged me to let them even it out, but I refused to let anyone but a trained professional near my precious bug-infested hair.

"We're quite the sight, aren't we?" Mom remarked.

"Where's Jim at?"

"He's afraid to go out in public with us."

"Why's that?"

"Thinks a cop is going to arrest him for battering his family."

"Hmm yes. I can see that."

IN PUNE, DURING NAPTIME at the BSSK orphanage when there was not much else for me to do except sweat, I went across town to visit a community center in a slum. I met twenty-five children there who came to the center for extra help with school, food, health, and dowries. They were gorgeous like kids in a Gap commercial. Their hair was crisply combed, their eyes open and round, and their teeth whiter than mine after I used those slimy tooth-whitening strips for a month.

The children there had very little and they knew it. The center had no electricity because of the blackouts, and the light that entered through the doorway shone gray on the rug in the middle of the room where the kids sat practicing the English alphabet.

"Tea?" the teacher asked me.

"Yes please. Namasté."

All twenty-five children sat duck-duck-goose style in a circle. Some were very small and some were engaged to be married. Some were both. The girls wore vibrantly colored dresses, and the boys' shirts were more firmly pressed than anything in my wardrobe. I sat among them along the circle's edge. In fifteen seconds they'd scurried around me, and I had become the circle's new center point.

Some of the boys who were training to be tour guides for foreigners spoke English, Spanish, and Japanese.

"Where from?" one of them asked me.

"U.S.A. Nebraska. There are farms and cows."

"We have cows."

"Where I'm from the cows don't walk on the highway."

"There are taxis there?"

"A few."

"We have taxis here."

"What is your favorite color, sir?" another boy in white asked.

"I like blue. Like sky blue."

The boy translated for the others and pointed up in the air at the dark brown ceiling.

"This is my sister. Lashka."

"Nice to meet you, Lashka."

She fiddled with her sari.

"I have three sisters. Two are from India. From Pune. Like you."

"What mean? Do they live India?"

"They used to. Twenty years ago. Now they live in U.S.A."

"Why?"

"They were adopted into my family."

"So they fly?"

"Yes. They flew."

"They like U.S.A.?"

"Yes, very much like U.S.A."

"They miss India?"

"Yes. Sometimes."

"They missing India family?"

"No, they don't have family in India anymore. Their parents died when they were young."

"Raj no have parents too."

Raj heard his name and looked over, nervous for a translation. When it came, he looked me in the eye, and I nodded in understanding. He nodded too.

Every year, 99.9997 percent of orphans in the world will not be internationally adopted. They need the kind of support and care the kids in Pune's slum community center receive. As for the children's parents, in one corner of the room are two 1960s sewing machines for mothers to use to make clothes both for their families to wear and to sell. The curtain in another corner of the room opens and closes all weekend long for health visits with doctors and nurses. They give advice to pregnant women on how to breastfeed their children so the infants get the right nutrients. They also dispense a 26-cent vaccine to prevent a child from dying of measles as well as a 6-cent solution to revive a sick, dehydrated baby dying from diarrhea. These simple supplies like vaccines and medicines are in high demand and low supply, so there's never any guarantee that children will receive what they need.

In addition to BSSK's community center, there are many other successful programs in Pune and around the world that work to keep families together and to keep kids with poor parents out of orphanages. One solution is to directly give poor families a few dollars a month. These cash transfers to parents or uncles or grandmothers or neighbors in charge of children can make a world of difference for a family's future. However, this does not solve the problem in the long term.

Recently, microcredit programs have emerged to help families take care of themselves. These little loans can consist of anything from a couple of chickens so a family can eat to a small sum of money so a mother can invest in basic supplies to create prayer beads that she will later sell outside temples.

Microcredit programs are also starting to be used to establish community daycare so poor parents can go to work during the day.

Without the help of a microcredit or charity daycare, a single mother would either have to forgo earning money to stay home with her children, leave her kids alone and vulnerable like Michelle and Jordan's mother was forced to do, or deposit her children in an orphanage, hoping to someday be able to go back and take care of them.

Some orphanages—such as BSSK—are run beautifully. But they should always be the last resort for children who still have parents or living relatives or community members who can take them in. There are too many other ways to take care of children that don't involve institutionalizing a generation of kids in poverty.

These inventive ways to educate, medicate, feed, and protect children are our best hope for stopping the wheel of poverty crushing orphans and vulnerable children. Without these caring interventions, children will live their whole young lives in orphanages deprived of the love and security of a family. If they're not institutionalized, the abandoned nine-year-olds of India's slums risk dropping out of school to get a job rolling cigarettes or having sex with tourists so they can eat. Later, if a treatable disease doesn't kill them first, these children will grow up uneducated, traumatized, and raising their own children in the same slum where their parents died.

Not every child is destined to win a golden plane ticket and escape poverty in faraway places. Only 0.0003 percent will, that's three in a million. International adoption is a wonderful option for these lucky few, but the millions of others left behind need options too.

As the children in the Pune slum prepared to leave the community center, they all huddled by the door slipping on their shoes. They babbled to each other in Marathi. Above the chitchat one boy with perfectly combed hair called to me, "All the best, sir . . ." I recognized him as Lashka's brother.

"All the best," I replied to the child who was about to go to his home made out of billboards and bed sheets.

"HOW WERE THE KIDS AT BSSK?" Dad asked when I called home.

"Refreshing, like an oasis."

"From all the chaos?"

"Yeah."

"I know. During my trip ten years ago, I only felt at home at the orphanage."

"Me too. That might make us a couple of weirdos, Dad."

"You're back in Bombay now?"

"Yep. Just waded through the monsoon to my hotel."

I was staying at an orange-carpeted hotel in Mumbai's West End, which got good reviews online as long as you weren't "in a room overlooking the hospital because you'll hear screaming all night." Room 413 had an excellent view of the hospital.

"Mom and I didn't stray too far away from the Taj Hotel where we stayed. They were filming a Bollywood music video out our window when we arrived."

"That's cool."

"Yeah—all night long. As you can imagine, your mother was thrilled when she was awakened by an electric sitar at 3 AM."

"I'd love to see some song and dance."

"Just be careful. I don't know if you've seen the news. There are bombings today in Ahmedebad not too far from Bombay."

"Thanks for worrying but I'll be fine, Dad."

There was no film crew when I arrived at the Taj Mahal Palace and Tower hotel—only two feet of water causing women to lift their saris above their knees. The building was attraction enough even without Bollywood superstar Shah Rukh Khan lip-syncing to a herd of 500 extras. The Arabian Sea splashed behind me. The building was a red brick fortress with cream portico windows that climbed up to the metallic dome, made of the same steel as the Eiffel Tower.

"Namasté," said a doorman in a plumed hat. Inside, a fairytale staircase lifted guests to their marbled rooms. The silence was broken only by the squeaking of my rubber-soled footsteps. The Burberry, Fendi, and Mont Blanc sales clerks moved around their stores in slow motion waiting for a tourist to buy a pen for the price of a lifetime supply of basmati rice. At the end of the hall I exited through an unguarded door and returned to the brown, muggy street.

"Namasté," said an armless man begging on a tattered cloth beneath the Louis Vuitton purse display window.

"Namasté," I replied and walked on.

A few months later in November 2008, as Americans were preparing their homes for the Thanksgiving meal, inhabitants of Mumbai were besieged by a series of terrorist attacks. Expensive hotels, restaurants, and other hot spots for richer Indians and foreigners were bombed. Crimson smoke puffed from the Taj Mahal Palace and Tower's portico windows. Nearly 200 people throughout the city's wealthiest havens were killed. The occasional abandoned stray shoe told the story of a tourist or businessman fleeing for his life at the Leopold Café. Puddles of blood stained the Taj's marble halls. Across the street from my own hotel, the hospital floor was cratered from the detonation of hand grenades.

THERE AREN'T MANY PHRASES in the English language more like a cold shower than the words "Global Political Economy" (GPE). It's the rhetorical equivalent of picturing your grandfather's nursing home sponge bath. However, in order to understand the hope for orphans in the world, you have to understand the political economics of our world.

Social causes that are easy to visualize, like the genocide in Darfur, polar bears drifting away on blocks of ice, and hungry kids in orphanages, often steal the spotlight from the economic core of the world's inequality problems. Bono writes a song to support AIDS awareness, and the American people donate $1.8 billion to the 2004 Boxing Day tsunami victims, and that's wonderful. If we ignored the world's immediate social ills until we erased global inequality, too many people would die before they had the chance to enjoy a renewed GPE. The challenge then is coupling our concern about social issues with the equally important economic ones.

Although they're probably not going to inspire a rock 'n' roll melody, international debt relief and trade policies affect international adoption every bit as much as AIDS, earthquakes, and tuberculosis do. The reason the structure of the world's financial regimes matters for children is simple: the broken state of the Global Political Economy begets poverty, poverty begets helpless parents, and helpless parents beget orphans.

Who are these helpless parents? The ones who can't afford to feed their children and have to relinquish them, or the parents who can't pay for malaria treatment so they die, leaving their children to fend for themselves. These parents are often members of the group Oxford economist Paul Collier calls the "bottom billion"—a billion people in the world who have to live on a dollar a day. A billion of people is difficult to imagine, so we don't. If we do imagine them, they seem so far away that many of us think, "Life costs less where they live," or, "They're just not working very hard."

The reality though is that food and medicine cost money no matter where you live. The cost of living may be higher in California or Rome, but the daily earnings of a Californian or Roman compared to the $1 day's earnings of a Taiwanese mother working to feed her family do not equate. Nor does the work she does to earn that $1. After seeing impoverished women climb a mountain every afternoon with four gallons of drinking water strapped to their backs, I dare anyone to say people in developing countries are lazy. Meanwhile, people like me pick up the phone to make a doctor's appointment and turn on the kitchen tap whenever they are thirsty.

The upsetting inequality in the world is not that a chair in a Yale-educated lawyer's office costs more than most farmers in India earn in ten years. There is nothing wrong with owning nice things. I like nice things. I paid an extra $200 for my laptop because of its color (black, like Carrie Bradshaw's on *Sex and the City*).

However, the unforgivable inequalities in the universe that incite the kind of hate that causes gunmen to light the Taj Mahal Palace and Tower hotel on fire are not our luxuries. They are the inequalities that end lives—the lack of food, lack of clean water, lack of vaccinations, lack of education, lack of shelter, lack of security.

There is some truth to another sentence typically spoken by the people who say "life cost less in Bangladesh" or "Africans are lazy." That is, "They don't know any different." They don't know what it's like to have clean water, to have a dependable food supply, to have sufficient means to care for their children. Even though the sentence is true, that does not mean it's right.

So how can the world close the gap and give everyone a fair chance? As much as I believe in the power of community centers and public health clinics and microcredit programs, those are mere treatments to alleviate the symptoms of poverty, but they are not cures. To eliminate poverty and solve the global orphan crisis we must aim higher and change the debt and trade rules of our global political economy. Currently, these rules are designed by and for the richest countries. Entire books are dedicated to how we can make the World Trade Organization and World Bank and International

Monetary Fund more fit to fight poverty, so I'm not going to try to say any more than that on the subject. I can already hear Mom wishing I would get on with it, so for her sake and yours, I will.

The big point is that to help orphans we have to do more than put a Band-Aid on their poverty. We must attack the roots of inequality. As I see it, the world will have passed the ultimate equality test the day international adoption becomes obsolete in every nation, when each country has the resources and systems in place to help its families and communities care for all their kids.

Right now, international adoption is giving poor countries a head start so that when they become financially capable, the infrastructure to adopt children locally will already be in place. Instinct tells me that my parents closed the global inequality gap a nanometer by giving my siblings a chance for a better life. However, when I examine the problem in more depth, it is evident that international adoption presents its own economic dilemma.

Some opponents of international adoption argue that the money it takes to adopt a child from a different country (up to $30,000) and raise that child in the United States ($100,000+) would be (should be) better spent caring for thousands of children in their home countries, like what is happening for the kids in Pune's community center. I understand the math, but the numbers are blurred by my feelings toward my siblings. I have trouble measuring the opportunity cost of my brother's and sisters' lives when I know they would not have survived in India.

Without Holt International and BSSK, Michelle's tuberculosis would have crippled and then killed her before her tenth birthday. Then Jordan, age five or so, would have been left alone to beg on the streets until he was kidnapped again. He probably would not have had to live in captivity for long though because his chronic sinus infection would have spread and done him in soon after he'd become a child trafficking victim. To be fair, Meredith might have lived had she stayed in India. She would have lived unloved in a crib for years, and when she grew up, she would have been unable to walk. What would her life be like in a country that had more respect for cows chewing their cuds in the middle of traffic than it did for abandoned lower-caste girls with physical abnormalities?

Yet my siblings' successes in the United States are the complementary cause of another child's misfortune somewhere else in the world. Their combined international adoption fees alone could have supported the people in a poor Indian village for years.

I guess my challenge now is to run a regression and come up with a neat supposition to settle the debate. But the thing is, even though I can lecture on and on about how to add up all the great ideas out there to end poverty, I still do not know how to calculate the economics of love. My feelings for my siblings are greater than logic. So I will conclude with a provocative cop-out quote from Mother Teresa, who is rumored on the Internet to have once said, "If you can't feed a hundred people, then feed just one." The question is, which one?

Chapter Eight

A TALE OF TWO KOREAS

TWO YEARS AFTER MICHELLE AND JORDAN arrived in the United States, we opened our house for the weekend to the woman who had made our family possible. Mom fixed Hamburger Helper on white disposable plates the night Bertha Holt ate dinner with us in Nebraska. Boxed dinners were about all my parents could muster back then. Within two years they had quadrupled the number of children under our roof. All of us were still young enough to show our age in fingers on two hands—4, 6, 9, and 10. It was autumn and we were back in school when the eighty-nine-year-old we called "Grandma" came to stay with us on her tour across the country raising money for orphans. She was petite enough to fit on the quilted twin bed Mom and Dad squeezed into the den beside our pre-Internet computer. Maybe she had the tolerance of a saint or maybe her hearing was blessedly on the fritz, but Grandma never seemed bothered by our noise and chaos.

During dinner Grandma Holt bowed her head down at a Styrofoam plate of Wagon Wheels, and each of us prayed our nightly

"Father, bless this food, Amen" around the table in ascending age order like a four-child sprint relay.

"Father, bless this food, Amen," said Meredith.

"Father, bless this food, Amen," said Jordan.

"Father, bless this food, Amen," said Michelle.

As soon as I mumbled my "Amen," it was forks up in frenzy.

Grandma ate graciously, like a woman who didn't know that she had started the domino effect responsible for saving half the lives sitting around the dining room table. I didn't know her power either, but my ignorance did not stem from an angelic humility. I was ten and oblivious to the bigger picture. Life with three orphans from the other side of the world was all I knew of normal and so that's what it was, what we were—normal. I didn't think about it. It sounds strange, like not wondering about a patch of purple grass growing in your backyard; but if the grass had always been purple, then there would be no reason to notice anything unusual.

AFTER DISCOVERING INDIA, I flew east to Korea, where I traded roles and spent the weekend at Grandma Holt's old house, which she and her husband Harry built when they returned to Korea to care for more children after their own adoption of eight. She was not there any more, but her daughter Molly Holt was, fifty years after the beginning of the Holts' work and eight years after her mother's death. I was there on the anniversary and was invited to the memorial service. All the Koreans around me were dressed in suits and *hanbok* dresses. My traveling T-shirt wardrobe was under-reverent but I tried to make up for it by putting on my nice sandals for the occasion.

The ceremony was all in Korean, but I understood the meaning nonetheless just as Molly Holt suspected I would. A twenty-voice choir in blue robes led the hymns for the seventy people who gathered on the hilltop. The singers ranged from children in wheelchairs to adults with Down syndrome. They all belonged to the same family but not in a Von Trapp lonely goatherd *odl lay hee hoo* type of way. Abandoned or relinquished by their parents who either couldn't afford to raise a child with special needs or wouldn't because it was not popular to be disabled in Korea, the handicapped singers lived together in group homes at the foot of a hill in Ilsan. It was the same hillside where Harry and Bertha Holt gathered their family one snowy winter and pitched a tent and insulated it with rice straw mats while Harry built the first Holt orphanage nearby. The tents were on the same hill where Harry and Bertha are buried. On this hill, the choir sang for Bertha.

Molly Holt had spent almost her entire adult life on that hill, living in a building her father built. The two-story home was now called Molly's House, and she shared it with the residents of the Holt Ilsan Center who needed the most assistance in living their daily lives. After the ceremony's final hymn and a kimchi lunch with rice and raisin cake dessert, I followed Molly to her home. We sat on folding chairs around the dining table and folded her laundry. She was still wearing the white-bloused, red-skirted *hanbok* she had donned for her mother's memorial service earlier that morning.

"It's new! A gift for today," she said.

I studied the picture frames on the mantel while she folded her underwear in squares. She didn't mind my looking, but it felt somehow wrong, like seeing Mother Teresa in a bikini. There were wedding photos of people who had grown up in Molly's House and the baby photos that followed of their pony-tailed kids. Hiding in a corner among all the colorful 8 × 10s was a faded black-and-white double portrait. It had been snapped at the Portland Airport in 1955. Harry was in white, Bertha in black. They had just been reunited and their eyes looked closed, either from exhaustion, the flashing press cameras, or a synchronized blink. The mutual expression, whatever its source, looked like a happy disbelief, one that neither Harry nor Bertha wanted to risk shattering by looking around in case it turned out not to be true.

"I met your mom when I was younger," I told her.

Molly moved on to balling her socks. "At a fundraising picnic?"

"She stayed at my family's house in Nebraska for a weekend. She even ate my mom's cooking."

"She thought of all the Holt families as a continuation of her own. That's why everyone called her Grandma."

"That's an awful large family," I said.

"She had about 50,000 grandkids. All ages and nationalities. Made no difference to her."

"Yeah."

"How did you feel in your family?"

"Just like a brother ought to I guess."

I felt that brotherly connection closest with Michelle. At 4:30 in the morning as Grandma Holt slept on her petite twin bed in the den down the hall, Michelle and I snuck down from our rooms to watch television in the family room. We did it every morning. There wasn't anything on worth watching. Just some old episodes of science experiments on *Mr. Wizard's World* and Dudley Do-Right riding a horse backward in *Rocky and Bullwinkle.* The selection got extra grim in the 5:30 to 6:00 AM timeslot when we were forced to choose between a show about a girl robot who slept in a closet and old Goofy cartoons on the Disney Channel that were scrambled like pornography because we didn't have a big enough cable plan. It didn't matter to us, though. We weren't sacrificing our sleep to be entertained. We did it to be together and start every day side-by-side.

"I felt like a normal brother for a long time," I went on. "Before things started falling apart. And then I guess I wasn't sure how to feel."

"Falling apart is normal, too, Aaron," Molly said. "When all eight of my Korean siblings were teenagers and Daddy had died, Mommy used to say to God, 'You got me into this mess and I expect you've got a plan to get me out of it.'"

"How'd that go for her?"

"All right in the end. But in the meantime she just kept living by her motto. You know, that all children are beautiful when they're loved." Molly picked up her laundry hamper and leaned it on her hip.

"I remember that."

"Yes, remember that."

The sky was one amorphous cloud and as the sun set, the color of the atmosphere changed from a hot gray to iris blue. I took the shortcut, a straight brick stairway up the lush hill, to the Holts' graves. Their tombstones, curved like granite tri-fold posters, were engraved with bilingual Bible verses and the words, "Beloved Grandfather, 1905–1964" and "Beloved Grandmother, 1904–2000."

Visiting the Holts' graves was only one of many reasons I chose to include Korea on my journey. My family's heritage is grounded in this land as well. My grandparents lived here. My youngest sister was born here. But there was more than that. Even though only one of my sisters left her umbilical cord in Korea, the lives of every one of my siblings are connected to Korea's history and culture, for it gave birth to international adoption today. I owe my life to that one-of-a-kind culture and history too, but I knew nothing of it. And I needed to understand it so I could take all that had fallen apart and start putting it back together again.

DURING THE 1970S, my grandparents Lenore and Meredith were stationed at the Eighth Army Post, just inside Gate 19 in Seoul, South Korea. Out her living room window, Grandmother could see army bunkers. There were holes in their walls caused by Japanese shelling in the early 1900s when the island nation's continent envy compelled it to colonize Korea. 1910 wasn't the first time the Japanese attacked the 85,000-square-mile peninsula dangling from the northeastern corner of China like an earring in the Yellow Sea. Japan's naval fleet had first invaded Korea in 1592, hoping to use the land as a base for conquering Ming China. The Japanese were defeated.

Although it might not seem evident at first glance, the 1590s conflict in that region directly affected the events in 1950s Korea, events that allowed the growth of international adoption. A few years after Korea drove Japan away, Christian missionaries arrived on Korea's shores. The missionaries had even less regard for the Korean way of life than the Japanese invaders did. To preserve Korea's ancient traditions, the kings of Korea's Joseon Dynasty installed an isolationist policy and excluded foreigners. This policy earned Korea the nickname "Hermit Kingdom," but it brought the people 200 years of uninterrupted peace and a genetic "purity" that Korean society valued.

Korea's isolationist peace wilted in the early twentieth century when the Japanese finally won control over the peninsula they'd coveted for centuries. From 1910 through the end of World War II, Japan forced Korean media to use the Japanese language, coerced Korean parents to give their children Japanese names, and stole the smartest Korean children to educate in Japanese schools. When 2 million Korean protesters gathered in peaceful opposition to their oppressors, the Japanese responded by killing 25,000 of the protesters and imprisoning 50,000 more.

Koreans rejoiced in August 1945 when Japan fell from the force of two atomic bombs and accepted the Allies' ultimatum of unconditional surrender. The euphoria of independence was short-lived though, because as soon as the Japanese were removed from Korea, the United States and the U.S.S.R. pulled out a map and divided the peninsula at the 38th parallel. The division was pure geopolitical symbolism. The two superpowers, already influenced by Cold War doctrines, wanted to assert their ideological dominance in the newly de-labeled map of the world.

By September 8, 1945, American and Soviet boots stomped on the streets of Seoul (in the South) and Pyongyang (in the North). The Korean resolve had withstood outside interference for centuries; it was now too feeble to fend off the country's latest invaders. The Korean people had already lost the sense of solidarity that had united them against Japan, just as the unity that Londoners experienced during the blitz in World War II began to unravel once the war was over and they could sleep in their beds again instead of in hammocks tied across the underground train rails. So, without the Koreans' consent, the country became a part of the Cold War battleground between the United States and the U.S.S.R.

The American and Soviet occupation of Korea was meant to last only until the United Nations could supervise elections there. When the time for elections came in 1947, the Soviets refused to comply with a unified countrywide election, and separate elections were held in the North and the South instead.

The South elected Syngman Rhee their new president. He took over from a U.S. general who believed that "Koreans and Japanese are all the same breed of cats." This did little to rebuild Korea's faith in foreigners. Meanwhile, the North elected Kim Il Sung, the father of North Korea's current "Dear Leader," Kim Jong Il.

In 1950, after Korea's elections were settled, U.S. President Truman's secretary of state, Dean Acheson, announced that South Korea was outside the U.S. defense perimeter and that its military would be on its own. He might as well have sent Dear Leader Kim Il Sung a formal invitation to invade the South. In late June 1950, it took North Korea four days to capture Seoul. Having stepped over the truce line, the North just kept going until they were in control of two-thirds of the territory below the 38th parallel.

The United States sent forces into Korea the day after Seoul fell, and fifteen other UN member nations joined the effort. A game of tug-o-war ensued with the South reclaiming Seoul and taking the North's Pyongyang before China showed up and tugged it back to Communism. In 1953, both sides called another truce, and the initial dividing line was restored. Millions of people died to preserve the status quo. The exact casualty count is not known, but it is estimated that the United States lost about 40,000 troops; South Korea—46,000; North Korea—215,000; China—400,000; and 2.5 million Korean civilians were killed or wounded. Nevertheless, from all this destruction and mayhem there was one change that enabled the Holts to follow their dream and firmly establish international adoption. The armistice agreement demilitarized two miles of mountains north and south of the line; that is still the demilitarized zone (DMZ).

I needed to walk this fragile line to appreciate its historic significance so I arranged a visit with a local tour company. On the way to the DMZ, the bus driver stopped at Freedom Bridge on the route to North Korea. It was the only bridge that remained between the two Koreas, and I got out to cross it in the opposite direction of the 130,000 prisoners of war who had raced across it to freedom half a century ago. My knowledge of the Korean civil war was limited to

*M*A*S*H* reruns. I had watched them before boarding the bus in Seoul bound for the 300-square-mile sliver of land between the South and the North. I would bet that most of America's knowledge of the Korean War was framed by the antics of Hawkeye and Hot Lips, even though three times more U.S. soldiers died in combat in Korea than in the American Revolutionary War.

On the drive to the bridge, an English-speaking South Korean woman who said her name was Wendy (which I suspected is spelled more like Yun Hee on her birth certificate) recited a Wikipedia-inspired history of the conflict.

"The conflict arose from the attempts of the two Korean powers to re-unify Korea under their respective governments in 1950," she read carefully from a jumbo index card that had been laminated for daily use in the propaganda war that today is being waged between the two sides.

Freedom Bridge's wooden slats were splotchy from sporadic raindrops that felt clean when they landed on my muggy skin. A six-foot-tall toy Korean soldier guarded the foot of the bridge on the south side. His oversized shoes were scuffed from children standing on them to take pictures with V-shaped fingers. Water droplets stuck to the paint on his black sunglasses and blue helmet that read "헌명."

I peered over the rail at a black pond of lily pads and white lotus flowers growing below. A chain-link fence dead-ended the bridge 100 meters in. Tattered flags, reunification ribbons, and handwritten Hangul letters to separated family members were tied to the chains. Through the fence, the undeveloped mountains of the North were serene like a sine wave. The raindrops multiplied and the Hangul bled.

At the border of the demilitarized zone I boarded a military bus operated by an American soldier. He issued me a red badge after I signed a disclaimer acknowledging that my visit "will entail entry into a hostile area and possibility of injury or death as a direct result of enemy action." The engine started, and I looked out the latched school bus window at the southern stretch of the DMZ. The zone was 155 miles wide and 2 miles high, buffering the peninsula's warring sides. The bus passed what *Sports Illustrated* magazine dubbed "the most dangerous hole in golf"—an Astroturf fairway enclosed by three sides of landmine rough. A stray shot from a 3-iron was enough to cause an explosion.

"Do not gesture to the North," the soldier commanded from the front of the bus. He held the back of a green leather bus seat for balance. "Do not wave. Do not point. Do not cross your eyes. I'm not in the mood to die today. Not here anyhow."

The bus stopped, and the other voyeuristic tourists and I piled out, instinctively staying in single file. A North Korean officer in olive uniform and red armband watched us through a giant pair of binoculars. We were at the DMZ junction where the South's border meets the North's. Five color-coded buildings—blue for South, khaki for North—dotted the dividing line. We entered the blue.

Inside, the walls were a glossy Smurf blue that lit up with a dozen flashbulbs. Two Southern guards stood stiff, legs apart, fists clenched, guns holstered, aviators affixed. The stockier man blocked the back door on the other side of which stood his Northern reflection, same in height, speech, and song. Identical if it weren't for the color of his shirt. We exited the way we had entered, and our footsteps disturbed the rocks that stopped at the concrete borderline, no taller than a chess piece. Sand filled the other side. The silent stare of a North Korean soldier four feet away reminded us not to cross.

I looked into his eyes and he looked through mine.

It was like a fifty-five-year-old game of Red Rover. I had the urge to yell, "Send Kim Jong right over!" But I wasn't in the mood to die today either.

Back in the bus our U.S. Army tour guide, still being careful not to point, directed our eyes to a 160-meter flagpole—three times the height of Cinderella's Castle at Disney World—poking the clouds on the North Korean side of the border. A red, white, and blue flag of the Democratic People's Republic of Korea, allegedly weighing 600 pounds, struggled to wave at the tower's peak. It would take a tornado to lift that thing in the air. One hundred and fifty-eight meters below slept a cobalt-roofed fantasy city built by the North to show the world how well its citizens lived. But no one lived there. The buildings were as empty as their glass-less window-frames. It was all pretend, part of an elaborate illusion responsible for the suffering of the country's 23 million people and the creation of my family.

FOLLOWING A COUPLE OF DECADES of relative peace, the U.S. Air Force dispatched my grandfather, a chaplain colonel, to Seoul in 1977. Although the ceasefire had been declared twenty-five years earlier, the two Koreas were still in a state of war and the U.S. military remained active in the region. A forty-nine-year-old Lenore crossed the Pacific with my grandfather and there, living across from the Korean army bunker, she observed a country in transition. The older Korean men and women still dressed in traditional Korean clothing, but the younger people dressed in the bell-bottomed fashion of the era. Some houses were quite nice, with gates or fences around them. But many people still lived in what she would call hovels made of pieces of metal or cardboard. Most meals were cooked outside the home on hibachis. Cars were small and driving was hazardous. If there were three lanes on the street, six cars would crowd into them.

While they were stationed in Korea, my grandparents met Father Keene, a Maryknoll priest doing Catholic missionary work there. One Christmas Eve service, Father Keene was delivering a sermon about the birth of the Son of God in a rank stable in Bethlehem when he noticed a group of Amer-Asian children standing in the doorway. The children told him they had no home but that they stayed together so they could take care of each other. Father Keene said, "I have a home and you can share it with me."

When my grandparents visited his home, two Korean women were washing children's clothes in a fishpond in the front yard. Since his Christmas Eve service, Father Keene had welcomed into his care many more children who were abandoned because of their foreign blood. After enduring the twentieth century's foreign suppression and enjoying 500,000 years of genetic seclusion beforehand, Korean society rejected the children of American G.I. fathers even though the babies' mothers were Korean. The half-white or half-black children tainted the purity of Korea's homogeneous bloodline, its *minjoksa,* the only thing in their country they still had some control over. The children who unhinged this control were considered non-persons and, in Korean society's eyes, deserved death.

When my grandparents told my mother the story of meeting Father Keene while she was in college, she had decided she would adopt a baby Korean girl. So when Meredith started first grade and there was no longer a baby at home, Mom and Dad filled out one more application for adoption. Dad was not an easy sell, but Mom pestered him like an eight-year-old daughter pestering her father for a new puppy and eventually got her way.

On their final application form, my parents repeatedly checked the "Yes" box on the special medical needs form. They still checked "No" for cerebral palsy. As history would have it, Yoo Jung Choi, the baby girl the Holt agency referred them, was diagnosed with CP and paralyzed on her left side. Her crawl was more a belly slither as she propelled herself forward with her right foot. And when she smiled, it was more an Elvis sneer as the right side of her lips curled up and her lazy left drooped down. With the care of her foster family and five physical therapy sessions a week, there was a chance she would outgrow the condition. My parents took it.

Around Christmas 1996, we got pictures of Yoo Jung Choi in the mail. I was in seventh grade and took the photographs with me to my junior high, PMS (Pound Middle School). I taped her picture inside my yellow locker next to the tidy grid of Alanis Morissette and Boyz II Men color ink-jet printouts. She was about one year old at the time, born eight weeks prematurely to an unmarried fifteen-year-old in the port city of Pusan. Her birth mother kept her pregnancy secret until she gave birth. Lying there in a white onesie with an inch of delicate black hair, Yoo Jung looked like a mini–Kim Jong Il the way bald Caucasian babies look like mini–Winston Churchills.

A DOZEN YEARS LATER, sitting on a mechanical toilet in Seoul, the capital of Yoo Jung's (Jamie's) motherland, I felt like I had traveled decades into the future. I was also feeling sick, and it was the American food's fault. I pushed the blue button on the remote attached to the toilet and a jet of cold water squirted up my butt. I was aiming for *flush* but *fountain* wasn't so bad.

I experimented with the other colored buttons stamped with Hangul picture-words. The white button with a top hat sticker changed the color of the toilet bowl. The pink pine tree button squirted me again but this time hit me somewhere it shouldn't. Aaah, lady parts. The green snowman finished the job with the flush I was looking for in the beginning. A xylophone jingle tinkled over the noise of vortexing water. It was like the song that played when you won a level of Super Mario Bros. while the screen flashed "Course Clear!"

It was the Korean alphabet that got me into this mess in the first place. All week I had been lured to Korean restaurants whose storefronts looked like oversized neon Christmas cards with their snowmen signs and evergreen forest special offers taped to the Plexiglas. Inside, I discovered that ordering dinner in a Korean restaurant is not like ordering in Paris, Florence, or Barcelona. You can't add an -eau, -zza, or -olé to an English word and cross your fingers that you guessed correctly when you're in Seoul. The best you can do is open with a well-rehearsed hello—"Ahn-nyong-hee-ga-se-yo"—and a sympathetic face.

On my first night in the city, eager for local flavor, I chose an authentic-looking eatery. I judged its authenticity by its back-alley location and the high number of Koreans sweating over hotpots behind the Christmas card window. My suspicion was correct. When I opened the door, the sweaty Koreans look at me in unison. A few pointed at me with their silver chopsticks. "Ahn-nyong-hee-ga-se-yo!" I waved. The waitress handed me a menu and pointed to an empty table in the center of the restaurant. The eight-page menu had no pictures or translations. Authentic.

The waitress, who was wearing a teddy bear apron, came to my table and said something I interpreted as "What would you like to eat?" but could have been "You need a haircut," for all I knew.

"Ahn-nyong-hee . . . uhm . . . hi," I started. "No English?" I tapped the menu.

"Eng-wish? Ah-nee-oh Eng-wish."

The other eaters all took a hotpot break to watch our exchange.

I could have pointed to a random item on the menu and prayed that when the plate came out it was an animal I recognized, except I had been a vegetarian for six years. It wasn't a moral diet. I didn't carry a PETA card and with all my skymiles I surely was not in the running for Mister-Low-Carbon-Footprint-of-the-Year. I did crave the soft white grease of a chicken finger on Friday nights, but I didn't like the idea of digesting things that used to wiggle. I was happy to wear them on my feet or use them to test the patina of my shampoo. I just didn't want them in my esophagus, that was all.

When I backpacked Europe after college, I made sure I knew how to say "vegetarian"—*végétarien, vegetariani, vegetariano*—in whichever country I visited. I never thought to learn how to say it in Hangul. Even if I had known the word, I'm not sure the teddy bear waitress would have known the concept. South Korea was a meaty place.

"Vegetarian?" I tried.

"Ah-nee-oh."

Miming time. I crossed my arms in an 'X' in front of my chest. "No . . ."

"No," she echoed, arms at her chest.

"Meat." I flapped my arms like a chicken.

The crowd loved this. The chopstick pointers were laughing.

"Ah-nee-oh."

"No . . ." Arms crossed again.

"No."

"Moooo?"

The whole restaurant was laughing.

"Ah-nee-oh."

I laughed along and pulled a small blue reporter's notebook and a hotel pen out of my bag. I flipped it open to an empty page and started to draw. A few other eaters got out of their seats and stood around my table. We played pictionary. I doodled a pig with a curly tail and then slashed an "X" through it. Murmurs of semi-understanding all around. Or perhaps they thought I wanted slaughtered hog. Then I drew an apple with a smiley face in the middle.

"Ah, Chae-shik! Chae-shik!" a girl wearing a Donald Duck T-shirt exclaimed.

"Chae-shik?"

"Chae-shik, chae-shik," the teddy bear waitress said as she wrote in her order pad.

"OK, chae-shik." I wrote that down in my blue notebook too for next time. "Gahm-sah-hahm-ni-da," I said appreciatively and bowed to them each individually.

My chae-shik meal was ready ten minutes later. It was a hill of white rice and brown mushrooms. Vegetarians are supposed to like mushrooms. But I was a bad vegetarian and sometimes wondered if I would rather have that greasy white chicken finger in my esophagus instead of a dirt-crusted fungus chunk. All my translators watched me when I slipped my silver chopsticks between my fingers and brought a mushroom to my lips. I swallowed it without chewing, and it went down like a slug on a Slip 'n Slide. "Mmmm."

I ate at authentic Korean restaurants for the next four days. Every time I ordered "chae-shik" I was presented ten minutes later with another dish of mushrooms and rice. On the fifth day, I caved and found the subway line to the international neighborhood of Itaewon, the capitalist product of fifty years of hosting foreign troops that offered homeland comforts to homesick soldiers.

Itaewon was only five stops on the subway from my group house, but I'd been resisting. Now, sitting on the train, my tongue sweated when I thought of feeding it something from back home. The Korean businessmen on either side of me watched the same television program on their cell phones. The phones had antennas that somehow received satellite signals underground at 40 miles per hour. They didn't use earphones, so I could share the soap opera drama. Just as a young male lead with a spiky hairdo started kissing his girlfriend, the light on the subway map turned on at the Itaewon stop and I alighted.

Back above ground, I rotated like a car on display. What I saw was the opposite of Chinatown. It was Americatown and I wanted it all. It was the neighborhood embodiment of my sister Jamie—Korean on the outside, All-American on the inside.

I began with a slice of Uncle Tom's Pizza. Then a burrito at a Tex-Mex restaurant named Tax-Max. And finally, a six-incher at Quizno's—no mushrooms, gahm-sah-hahm-ni-da very much. Full and happy, I walked around Itaewon. American men and women in gray ARMY T-shirts drank beer at sidewalk tables. Their colleagues on duty in khaki camouflage patrolled the area to prevent lapses in judgment. I followed the patrol up a steep red-light street called Hooker Hill and then down the adjacent pink-lit street called Homo Hill. American men and women in gray army T-shirts drank beer on the sidewalks of Homo Hill, too. The patrolmen waved to those they knew.

As I walked back toward the subway I saw it—an orange and pink Dunkin' Donuts sign. There was not a single Hangul character on the storefront, but it still looked like Christmas. I went in and took a raspberry-filled glazed donut to the register.

"You skinny. Take two," the cashier told me. I did. They tasted like every cliché you've ever heard in a TV commercial—the finger-licking sweet glaze melting in my mouth. Finally I let out an authentic "Mmmm." I walked back to the subway and on the ride home my insides growled louder than the businessman's television-cell-phone speaker next to me. Uh-oh. Two more stops.

I speed-walked back to my ancient group house and beelined for the toilet that did everything but. Twenty minutes later I pushed the blue water squirt button once more for good measure and pulled up my pants.

Compared to the achievements of South Korea in the past fifty years, from its rise onto the global stage to the way South Koreans care for their orphaned children, North Korea is living in what Charles Dickens would have labeled its "winter of despair." But looking in history's rearview mirror, it is sadly curious that North Korea has not struck the spring of hope for its people and orphans by now.

The global events of 1989 and onward demonstrate that nobody can do Communism quite like North Korea can. First, the Berlin Wall was pulled down and East Germany reunited with West Germany. Then the Soviet Union dissolved. Communist China manufactured itself as a global king of capitalism. And after forty years of ruling as "The Great Father" of North Korea, Kim Il Sung died. I was eleven when Kim Il Sung was buried beside the great bastions of Bolshevism, but even in my early teenage years I could have predicted what the experts did: the state of North Korea will collapse.

Yet the country still stands (albeit hunched, frail, and lonely) today, two decades after its European counterpart fell. North Korea and East Germany are parallel lands in many ways. They were both born in the dust of World War II, in the first dark light of the Cold War. They were both halves of a homogeneous dichotomy. And they had both dismissed the centuries when they were whole, the time before a cardinal direction prefixed their name in an atlas.

Unlike in Germany, though, a longstanding tradition of totalitarian regimes was not new in Korea. For millennia, Korean society operated under the Confucian way of life, which is governed by a series of dominant-submissive relationships. Old to young, husband to wife, father to son, ruler to subject. Due to these ingrained power dynamics, life for starving North Koreans in the shadow of "The Great Father" Kim Il Sung's fat belly was compatible with the same Korean lifestyle that had existed 1,500 years before Karl Marx learned to write.

In Communism, just as in Confucianism, every person has a place in the everyday hierarchy to preserve societal harmony. Kim Il Sung and his son Kim Jong Il capitalized on this twin custom to achieve their own idol status and maintain control of Communist North Korea even after the rest of the Reds in the world lost their grip. The importance of preserving the Confucian/Communist harmony is so embedded in the Korean psyche that in spite of the view the Western world has of Kim Il Sung and Kim Jong Il, the North Koreans have continued to worship them—an outcome neither the experts nor I could have predicted when I was eleven.

It is simple to mistake harmony for happiness, but the two are not listed together in a thesaurus. Beethoven's *Moonlight Sonata* is perfectly harmonious, but it's not the kind of song you'd want playing at a bachelorette party. North Korea's harmony is sad with lots of repeat signs. A quarter of the country's budget is used on its military while hundreds of thousands of its citizens are forced to quit work and school to roam the mountains and sea in search of food. The country's malnutrition is not just the result of North Korea's government prioritizing guns above grains. Until the 1970s, the military-minded North outpaced the South in per capita income. Although South Korea's export economy eventually surpassed North Korea's, the North was doing all right until its Communist comrades abandoned ship in the '90s, and it became the world's Hermit Kingdom once more. Without the Soviet Union selling goods at Socialist-friendly prices, isolationist North Korea struggled. Since the division at the 38th parallel, the U.S. Congress has passed ten separate sanctions of commercial and financial transactions between the United States and North Korea.

The shortage of trading partners not only stunts North Korea's economy but also makes it vulnerable to shocks in domestic food supply. Here's how. If Country A isn't able to trade with Countries B, C, or D, when Country A runs out of food, the inhabitants of Country A will starve. Even when the weather's good for farming, trade sanctions disadvantage North Korean agriculture by cutting access to the fuel and fertilizer its farmers need to make their land arable. Forced to be self-reliant, North Korea instated a do-it-yourself fertilizer policy for winter. The frozen human waste from every public toilet in the country was chipped loose, set out to melt in the spring sun, mixed with ash, and then spread across the countryside. The makeshift mixture is called *toibee* and, according to a 2009 *Washington Post* report, "Barring a miracle, it won't work"—merely sink the country in more deep shit.

No one knows for sure because North Korea isn't telling, but as a consequence of the country's food vulnerability, somewhere between 1 and 3 million North Koreans died of starvation in the mid-1990s when an alternating plague of droughts and floods destroyed the harmonious country's crops. On the optimistic end of international NGOs' death toll estimates, one in twenty North Koreans starved to death. At the estimate's worst, provided by North Korea's former agriculture diplomat Kim Dong-Su, who fled the country in the late 1990s: one in seven. North Korea appealed for help to the World Food Programme (WFP), but it was too little too late. Even today, with WFP operations more routinely in place, most North Koreans are only allotted 350 grams of food a day. The World Health Organization recommends 700 grams a day to sustain life.

When the aid arrives, about a third of it will find its way into the hands of the Pyongyang elite to trade for a profit, and the rest will be scattered among the starving in harmonious hierarchy. In the great Confucian tradition, much of that hierarchical structure is organized along family bloodlines. Orphans, therefore, are outliers of the system and are barely privy to the country's already weak support skeleton. They will suffer the most.

In Sinuiju (a town pronounced Shin-ju on the northern edge of North Korea), the poorest parents will drop off their newborns on the doorsteps of childless neighbors, hoping they will feed their child even though they know the neighbors probably cannot. Abandoned babies who can't be raised by someone in the community or extended families end up in one of Sinuiju's orphanages, which serve more as hospice homes for children.

In November, the skin on a Sinuiju orphanage director's hands is cherry and chapped. The temperature in his office is literally freezing. He keeps it that way so he can keep the babies' room warmer. It is warmer but more spine chilling than the inside of a lion pen. The room, stuffed with babies, is mute. They're not sleeping. Every child's eyes are open, following your every step, silently willing your feet in his or her direction.

They want to be touched but won't cry for it because they have already learned that crying is a waste of energy. Crying does no good when there is nobody there to pick them up. Harry Holt understood the human need for contact. Whenever he met a lifeless child like the children at the Sinuiju orphanage, he would unbutton his shirt and slip them in, skin to skin, like a kangaroo and her joey.

When you bend over a crib and pick up a baby, it feels like you are holding air and that's when you feel it, the weight of helplessness. But the helpless sorrow is not the child's whose premature death was preordained from birth. The helplessness is yours because you know that the minute will come when you will have to let go of the baby boy you're holding—and when you do let go and board that thirty-minute flight to Seoul with its singing toilets, television cell phones, and cheese pizza without him, he will die in his crib and you couldn't, didn't change his fate.

North Korea's future is about as predictable as driving drunk without a seatbelt. Maybe you'll pull in safely to your garage at the end of the journey or maybe you'll be dead in a five-car pileup on the Interstate. There are signs of deterioration. The North Korean children of the 1990s whose lives and bodies were shaped by famine are five inches shorter than their South Korean peers. Famine also misshaped the young generation's minds, and now a quarter of the age-eligible recruits for the North Korean army are disqualified because of mental retardation caused by malnutrition. The demand for food has also caused markets, Communism's antithesis, to sprout up. Kim Jong Il has ordered the police to clamp down on them, but many in his force are defecting, corrupted by their own needs.

The holes in the harmony still might not be enough to end the suffering of the country's population of 23 million. North Korea should have collapsed four times by now and yet it survives. Supported by a Confucian sensibility, people continue to revere their "Dear Leader" in sunglasses despite the cruelty of his rule. Outside North Korea, world leaders, comforted by the safety of the status quo, continue to placate the Hermit Kingdom and prevent any abrupt changes.

Even Seoul (in spite of the tattered flags, reunification ribbons, and handwritten Hangul letters tied to the Freedom Bridge) seems to support North Korea's survival. When it considers the financial costs of reunifying two states and the societal burden of annexing an unskilled, unfed, and unloved population, South Korea wants North Korea back about as much as an older brother with embossed business cards wants to take in his felonious little brother with nothing but scrappy baggage.

A FEW WEEKS BEFORE I FINISHED seventh grade, we got clearance from the South Korean government to get Jamie. Mom traveled overseas to bring her Korean daughter home. Looking out the window at the Lincoln Airport, Meredith spotted Mom and Jamie's plane taxiing on the runway home from Seoul. "They're coming in Gate 3. They're coming!" she sang, gripping the bottom of her denim skort (a blend of skirt and shorts that was fashionable in the '90s). I came from behind and picked her up. She was seven but had the body of a four-year-old. Mine was the body of a boy in puberty, unsure and swollen. My gold-rimmed glasses were huge on me like the XL blue shirt that nearly covered the bottoms of my white jean shorts. Michelle and Jordan joined us by the gate. Dad held the camcorder.

Mom was the first person off the plane. It looked like she hadn't combed her hair in a week, but she had bothered to apply a new layer of cranberry lipstick. Her pink blouse was untucked from her high-waisted jeans. Jamie, who until then had been known as Yoo Jung Choi, sat in a blue papoose and clung with both hands to Mom's breasts.

"Hi guys," she said and crouched to the ground with her arms open for her other four children to fit inside. "Here's your baby sister."

Jamie, at fourteen months, looked around at her new family smothering her from all sides.

"Why don't we get outta the way," my dad suggested. The seven of us were pow-wowing in the path of everyone else off-ramping the plane. Pregnant-looking men with prints of sports cars on their shirts and AquaNet-loving women with pictures of hearts and cows on theirs walked past our tribe. Some looked at us in bewilderment and others looked away in irritation. Why they seemed annoyed, I was not sure.

Looking above the camcorder lens at my dad, Mom said, "I'm really tired. Don't I look like it?"

He responded with a laugh.

"So what do you think?" she asked the rest of us.

"Nice. She's little," Jordan said.

Michelle combed Jamie's fine black hair with her fingernails.

Meredith reached up for Mom's hand. "Mother, did she keep on blabbling?"

"She's quite a happy little talker."

"Like me, Mom? Like me like me?"

"Yeah. Kinda like you, Jordan."

"Sit, sit sit, Mom, sit," he said.

"I've been sitting for 30 hours." She shook her bangs to one side. "Sitting I don't need to do. I need to go to sleep."

Over the noise of Jordan's talking, Mom pointed Jamie's face toward the camcorder. It was cute and round, pale and pristine. A few white baby teeth poked through the dark of her mouth. She had sideburns. You would never know she was born with cerebral palsy. "This is daddy."

"Back off, Jordan!" I yelled in the background.

"Aren't you happy?" Dad said to Jamie, ignoring his sons.

"Calm down, guys. I know it's exciting," Mom said.

"You gotta be takin' a picture, Michelle. Take a picture."

"She's not crying," Michelle said, ignoring Jordan.

"No, she really doesn't."

"You gotta be takin' a picture."

"Tickle, tickle," Meredith sang. "Mother, is she ticklish?"

To find out, eight hands reached for a part of Jamie's body to tickle. She scrunched her face like she was filling her diaper.

Screams of "Hi!" and "Aaah!" boomed in another corner of the four-gate airport terminal. Someone else's family was reuniting as ours was being born.

We were all still tickling our new sister, who squirmed in Dad's arms. "OK. Stop," he told us. We backed off. She stuck her tongue out through a few white baby teeth poking through the dark of her mouth. He touched his stalky finger to her pebble nose. "Let's go home."

Chapter Nine

WHITE BOY IN A DARKENING FAMILY

THE SUMMER AFTER JAMIE CAME HOME, Jordan won the gold medal in roller skating limbo at The Skate Zone, defeating the Brazilians, Russians, and Chinese. Most of the adoptive families in Lincoln were there. With children from so many different countries, it was almost like a little United Nations summit.

"I won! Aaron! I won!"

"Won what?" I asked even though I had seen the whole thing. Standing on the wall of the skating rink, I saw how in each round Jordan hunched lower and lower under the pole until at last he widened his Gumby legs in an almost perfect split and rolled under as casually as if he were sitting in a wheelchair. Meanwhile, I'd knocked the pole off its posts on my first try.

"Limbo! I won loller-skating limbo!"

"Oh, nice jo . . ." I started but he was already skating off to tell Dad, who was sitting down with Jamie on the fuchsia carpet.

"Dad! I won loller-ska . . ." his voice trailed.

Mom's voice filled Jordan's void. "Hey White Boy—how about you take Meredith out for a couple laps."

I can't remember the first time Mom called me "White Boy." I guess that's how long the nickname's been around. Over time the name grew to be a term of endearment in the family but that was never its original intent. Mom's goal wasn't to dent my self-esteem. She knew I could handle it and wouldn't have said it if I couldn't. By calling me White Boy, she gave my brother and sisters something to make them feel special. Like they belonged to a special club, one that, although I might get everything else I wanted, I could never join.

"Give me your hand, Meredith," I said. She did and we shuffle-skated together around the edge of the rink so she could hold on to the wall for extra support. An Amy Grant song played on the speakers. "Every heartbeat bears your name."

A pair of Guatemalan kids whizzed by. A Korean girl biffed it and put her arms up in the air waiting for her Ukrainian friend to hoist her up. Michelle practiced her backwards skate a few meters ahead.

"Go Meredith!" Michelle shouted, looking back at us inching along. "You having fun?"

"Yep! I like it here."

We all did. And not only because of the flying sensation of eight wheels beneath our feet or the high likelihood that we could convince Mom and Dad to buy us each jumbo pretzels with cheese from the rink's snack bar for lunch. Although those were nice perks. Most of all, we liked the subconscious feeling that we were special and were surrounded by other special families, even though all of us were too young to articulate it. As far as we knew, we were normal like the families outside the skating rink, just another purple patch of grass on the Nebraska prairie. When the music stopped, we unlaced the skates and put on our shoes. As we walked through the parking lot, the phantom sensation remained—the feeling of flying.

~

Living in an international household with five kids of varying skin colors was never the problem everyone seems to expect it to have been. Inside, life was fine—a happy multiracial harmony. When I got mad at my sisters, it wasn't because I was feeling racist that day. They probably just ate the last Oreo. The problems only started when we walked out the front door.

Michelle's wet black ponytail was shiny like a seagull's feathers after an oil spill. She wore a pink swimsuit as she ran barefoot on the sidewalk out of her swimming lesson. Rolling open the door to the new minivan, she remembered how angry Dad had been at Jordan when he squirted a ketchup packet on the floor mat. So Michelle covered every square inch of the seat with her beach towel to avoid dripping chlorine water on the pristine upholstery.

An average married couple will buy his and hers bathrobes for their fifteenth wedding anniversary. My parents bought each other companion seven-seater vans to drive our family around town. Dad's Buick could squeeze four kids but not the five we now had with Jamie at home. And Mom had sold her dream green Jaguar years before in exchange for a navy blue minivan the same shape as a dust buster vacuum cleaner.

"What's a nigger?" Michelle asked when she clicked her seatbelt.

Mom turned off the radio, which she had tuned at high volume to the classical music station because she liked it, but mainly because we hated it. "Who called you a nigger?"

"How'd you know somebody called me . . ."

"What asshole called you a nigger?"

I had never heard Mom use either of those words before and definitely not in the same sentence. So I awkwardly looked out the window inventorying the slight differences between the houses on the street—*that one has a purple trim, their Christmas lights are still up in July.*

"A boy in swimming class, Mom," Michelle said as if she were in trouble.

"Asshole parents then. Ignorant asshole parents. You're not even black—you're Indian!" She honked the horn at the air. *Two plastic deer instead of just one, no basketball hoop in the driveway.* Jamie started kicking the back of the driver's chair from her baby seat. "Listen all of you. Quiet, Jordan! Listen." *Ferns under the windowsill versus hydrangeas.* "You too, White Boy." I turned from the window to face her. It might seem like an odd time to use my racially inspired nickname, but by then the term had become so ingrained in my family's everyday speech that it held about as much meaning as a word like "pookie."

"The next time some idiot picks on you because your skin is dark or you're adopted and they want you to feel bad because they think you're different, then I want you to look them in the eye. Look at them and say, 'I have beautiful brown skin and a family who loves me.' Say it now, Michelle."

She murmured it.

"Say it like you believe it next time, OK?"

IN SEOUL, I ARRIVED BACK AT my 500-year-old traditional Korean guesthouse from a 600-year-old Korean palace at midnight. Mom was waiting for me on Skype 15 hours behind my time. "Do you love Korea like I do?" she asked.

"It's stunning. Very happy here. Speaking of, when did Jamie turn into a knockout? I mean, she's always been pretty but I saw the pictures from her birthday party on Facebook. Wow."

"Puberty is her friend. But she's turning into a valley girl and I am too old to have two teenagers." She sounded tired.

"Aah, how is Meredith?"

"She wants to quit beauty school. I'm sure secretly she wants to join the boyfriend in Texas."

"Hell no," I said. "She can't keep quitting whenever something doesn't go her way."

"You need to tell her that for a change. I said those exact words to her four times already today."

"OK. I'll write her an email . . . for a change."

The next morning, sipping tea on a pillow on the ground at the breakfast table, I spoke with a German couple who were also staying at the Korean guesthouse. I started telling them about Grandma Holt's ceremony on the Ilsan Hill. They put down their chopsticks, and the husband explained that they were thinking about adopting an Asian baby because his wife was infertile. When she first found out she couldn't bear children, she became clinically depressed and sought treatment. When they applied to adopt a German child, they were declined because of her mental health records. Their only hope for a baby was to adopt from another country, but they were hesitant because they weren't sure it was right for a child to be raised in an interracial family.

I had heard their concerns before. The international adoption debate often centers on the question of how a child develops with parents who look different from him or her. It's an inane debate when you consider the other option, which is letting the kid rot in an orphanage, but somehow the debate persists.

To ease their fears, I told the German couple the story of Meredith, who was the first of us to get to use Mom's advice from that afternoon in the minivan. For years after her many reconstructive foot surgeries, Meredith had to wear steel-toed shoes that sculpted the bones in her feet the way that braces straighten your teeth. When she was four, she was about to go down the slide at the neighborhood park when an older boy pushed her aside and muttered, "Freak." Cutting in front of her, he sat down at the top ready to slide and Meredith climbed back up behind him as if she was waiting her turn.

"Mom, should we go stop him?" I asked.

"Not just yet, Aaron. I want to watch this."

Then, as if following cues from Mom's mental screenplay, Meredith gave the boy a steely kick in the back with her orthopedic shoe and boomed, "I have beautiful brown skin and a family who loves me!" for the whole playground to hear as he slid in pain.

"That's my little girl." Mom beamed.

"See that. That is what we are concerned about," the German would-be father commented on my anecdote.

"No, Klaus. You are missing the moral of the story," his wife said. "It is not being important what a race is inside of the family. They are not caring. The problems we see is starting when people outside the family is stupid."

Klaus shifted on his pillow seat. I assumed his butt cheeks were sore from sitting on the ground for too long. Mine were.

"OK but I am not wanting our daughter to endure this ignorance," he said and looked to me as if he wanted me to give his regards to Meredith.

"If your adopted daughter is strong enough to live without parents to take care of her, chances are, when she has parents like you who do, she'll be able to survive some taunting."

"Like your sister . . ."

"Yeah. Mostly." I stirred my tea and changed the subject.

When I returned from breakfast to my silk-screened room with a one-inch-thick mat for a bed on the floor, I sat back down and checked my email to see if Meredith had replied to my note about her dropping out of school. Her five response emails said that she wasn't moving to Texas. Her boyfriend was breaking up with her. And she wasn't going to leave bed. Not for two days at least. Well, maybe to pee.

I replied with one sentence I should have said years before. "Find your spirit . . . you lost it somewhere." The week before this exchange I had hugged the kids in BSSK goodbye. I felt the life-fire that blazes in orphaned children and keeps them going. Anyone who has ever met one of these kids will say they were touched by the magic inside them. To me, Meredith's survivor fire used to be hotter than any other child's. But I'd forgotten it and so had she. It took this journey to make me remember, and I wanted her to remember too.

EVEN BEFORE JAMIE'S ADDITION to the family, we were ruled by routine for years. Everything in our lives had a pattern. Every meal, activity, outfit, all of it. My parents depended on predictability the way flying geese rely on their *V* formation. It increased our family's chances of survival. The digital clock in the minivan told the story of our family on Saturday, on every Saturday for years:

9:10 AM: The van pulled out of the house early in the morning after Mom and Dad had fed everyone their choice flavor of toasted Eggo waffle. We drove to drop Michelle and me off at piano lessons.

9:45 AM: The van dropped Jordan off at tae kwon do while Michelle and I lied to our piano teacher about how many hours we'd practiced our scales and arpeggios that week. Meredith and Jamie stayed buckled up in the van, coloring photocopies of Pumbaa from *The Lion King* coloring books and eating Honey Nut Cheerios out of the box with their hands.

11:30 AM: Jordan finished kicking out his extra energy at the air and got back in the minivan. The engine restarted and drove back to pick Michelle and me up from our piano lessons.

11:45 AM: Michelle and I were waiting on the stoop out in front of the piano studio as the van arrived fifteen minutes late.

Noon: Depending on whether it was the first, second, third, or fourth Saturday of the month, we went to the children's museum, Nebraska history museum, natural history museum, or the zoo. We had memberships in all of them. We knew every family deal in town and abused them as often as we could. We scoured the coupon section for buy-one-get-one bubble bath. Then we discovered that kids eat free on Tuesday at Grisanti's Italian Kitchen, so we started eating there week after week until they finally had to change the rules. And when we bought strawberry yogurt, we bought the gallon tubs because we knew we would scrape the bottom of the bucket days before it expired.

4:00 PM: The best deal of all was the library. We each had our own card. Even tiny Jamie. I was in the history section looking for books about the sinking of the *Titanic* that included plenty of pictures. Michelle was by the magazines making a stack of back issues of *Seventeen* and *Mad* to take home for the week. Jordan was rummaging through the card catalogs and the microfiche machine and the koi fishpond but was nowhere near the books. Meredith was looking for the latest *Amelia Bedelia.*

5:15 PM: The new shipment at TJ Maxx discount clothing store arrived on Fridays so we tried to be some of the first to flick through the merchandise. The store clerks at TJ Maxx (and every store in Lincoln for that matter) trailed Michelle and Jordan; they had been trained to believe that one of them was going to stuff a pair of socks down their pants because they had dark skin and that's what their managers and television shows told them dark-skinned people were prone to do. "How about this one?" Michelle asked me, holding up a shirt of the Pillsbury doughboy. "It's Poppin' Fresh!"

I read aloud the T-shirt. "Tummy Poke-finger."

"See it's in a Tommy Hilfiger design."

"I see. But I don't wear Tommy Hilfiger."

"Ugh, you don't get it, White Boy. But you need this shirt."

"You're sure it's cool?"

"This one too."

6:00 PM: While Dad refueled the van at the gas pump outside the station, the rest of us invaded the candy aisle inside. If we had been "good" (not called names, thrown a tantrum, or vandalized any walls) Mom bought us each one pound of candy as a reward. I opted for fruity candy, Michelle for chocolate, Meredith for Sweet Tarts, Jamie got animal crackers, and Jordan was usually disqualified and got nothing.

6:15 PM: The garage door rolled up and the van rolled under. Dad parked and managed to not hit and upset the balance of the dozens of bikes and balls tightly lining the perimeter of the room. Mom and Dad lingered in the front seat for a moment to recuperate. "One more day closer to having the house back to ourselves, dear," Mom said.

"Only 6,136 more," Dad replied.

Our routine wasn't restricted purely to activities outside the house. That was just on Saturdays. On Sundays routine was confined to the home.

"Jordan, this afternoon you've got garbage duty," Mom said standing by the staircase with all the cleaning supplies lined in a row on the bottom step. "Bathrooms for Michelle." She handed over the yellow rubber gloves and a sponge with stains that didn't leave much to the imagination. "Meredith, I just want you to clean your room. I haven't seen your floor for weeks."

"What's Aaron have to do?" Jordan flapped open a folded garbage bag.

"He's going to dust. I'm going to vacuum. And Daddy and Jamie are going to videotape."

"I want to dust."

"You got to last week, Michelle." Mom looked directly into the camera lens. "It's important to have well-rounded indentured servants. OK, troops. Roll out. Spit spot!"

I started with the elephant collection in the living room. Mom had collected hundreds of Indian elephants ("not the African type, you can tell by the ears") ever since Meredith's arrival. They were carved from sandalwood, marble, bone, and one that looked like ivory, which I hoped was a knockoff and not a cruel irony. The Indian elephant collection was only a small part of Mom and Dad's international heritage décor. There was the opal hutch and dressing screen from Korea in the living room where no one ever spent any time. Hand-painted blue Hindu gods danced in a circle with forty mortal women on nearly every wall in the house. And a charcoal kimchi pot sat beside the fireplace. Just little things to make my siblings feel more connected to the cultural roots of their home countries.

"You don't make for very exciting video right now, Aaron," Dad said as I picked up one elephant at a time and dusted the surface with a brown feather duster Mom had originally bought as an accessory to the French maid costume she wore one Halloween before she had children. "Let's go see Michelle, shall we Jamie?"

Jamie clapped her hands. "Shmell!" It was her pronounceable nickname.

A purple Minnie Mouse shirt was reflected in the bathroom mirror Michelle was cleaning with the sponge. Her feet on the counter straddled the pit of the sink so she could reach the high parts.

"Hi Dad."

"Michelle, what's your favorite part about cleaning?"

"Nothing."

"Is the bathroom the worst duty?"

"Yep."

"Well . . . sing a little happy song. You know, whistle while you work." Dad began whistling the melody to their song.

"*Michelle . . . my belle,*" she sang along, wonderfully off-key.

"Where did you learn to sing so bad?"

"Hey! I'm not a bad singer."

"You are the worst! You couldn't even keep in tune to a Janis Joplin song."

"Who's Janis Joplin, Dad?"

"Oh, brother."

"I'm not your brother!" Michelle giggled—high, rapid, and unrelenting.

"At least you have a great laugh."

"That I do." More giggling. "That I do."

"OK, keep up the cleaning. We're gonna keep filming."

"See ya, Dad."

"Hi Meredith." The door to Meredith's bedroom opened, pushing aside the mound of debris like windshield wipers trying to brush away six inches of snow after a blizzard. "This doesn't look like cleaning to me. Jamie, do you see cleaning that needs to be done here in Meredith's room?"

"Bazaal," Jamie babbled.

The camcorder panned down to the toys and dresses and Barbie convertible with two Kens in the front seat going for a joyride with the top down. Then back up to Meredith, who sat on the edge of her bed surveying her mess.

"Looking at it is not going to make it go away, Meredith. And I'm no Mary Poppins with a spoonful of sugar. You've got until the end of QT to finish."

"QT" was the quick way to say "Quiet Time" around the Eske house, which was the sweet way to say imprisonment. After all the toilets were scrubbed and trashcans were emptied, we were sent to our rooms to entertain ourselves for the rest of the afternoon. Today, I'd probably appreciate the chance to just *be* for a few hours, but as a kid it was torture.

"How much longer?" I asked Michelle through the heating vent that connected our bedrooms. We lay on the floor talking through the thin metal slats that separated us.

"We got awhile. The sun's up high still."

"What are you doing over there?"

"Organizing my dresses by color and length."

"Where does your old Cinderella costume go?"

"I'm wearing it."

"Really?"

"Yeah. Are you wearing your Halloween costume?"

"No!"

"Why not?"

"It's back in Mom's closet."

"You were an ugly girl anyway, Aaron."

"Thanks. You, too."

"I wish I had a closet like Cher in *Clueless*."

"Yeah. With a computer to choose your outfits for you."

"How much longer now in QT?"

"The sun didn't move yet."

"What are Butch and the Babes doing back there?"

"The Babes are grazing. Butch is checking one of them out."

"Do bulls check out cows?"

"Yes! I'm watching it right now out my window."

"Which cow is it?"

"The skinny one."

"The one with brown freckles on her face?"

"Yep. That one."

"We're never getting out of our rooms."

"Never."

"OK. Go hang up your dresses."

"Check back in ten minutes?"

"Cool."

On weekdays, Mom took us older kids to school and Dad took Jamie to daycare before they both went to work. Mom arranged her schedule so when our school bell rang, she clocked out and headed home in her blue minivan. We took the bus or walked to meet her there.

As soon as we came inside the house, we hung our coats on hooks, unpeeled a strawberry Fruit Roll-Up, and opened our binders to do the day's homework at the dining table. Mom sat at the head of the table teaching Michelle how to use a ruler and quizzing Jordan on his fourth grade spelling words.

"Twinkle."

"T–W–I–N . . ."

On Mondays, Tuesdays, and Thursdays when Dad brought Jamie home for dinner, we all gathered back at the dining table. We took turns telling each other about our days like employees in a staff meeting. Then it was upstairs for bath time, book reading, and bed.

Wednesday was Mom and Dad's date night when Gina (who lived in our basement) spiced up our nightly routine. While we stayed in eating frozen pizzas and sneaking in episodes of *Melrose Place,* our parents got Chinese food and walked around a bookstore perusing. Even breaks in the repetition were repetitious.

The only item on the weekly agenda that was not predictable was which movie Dad would rent for Michelle and me to stay up late and watch with him on Friday night. Mom would make us popcorn and then go to bed early to make up for the hours of sleep she had missed during the week.

FOR A WHILE, JAMIE'S CRIB took turns in each of our bedrooms until Mom and Dad moved our family to the Water Tower house where we could each have our own 1,000 square feet. A lot had happened since Jamie came home and we dug out the moving boxes from storage that we kept around because chances were we'd be moving again soon. Gina, the woman in our basement who acted as our parents' part-time nanny/counselor/lifesaver, was engaged and going to live in her own house. Dad's law firm had an ugly split, and he quit to work for a judge in town. And Michelle had become a teenager and trouble was brewing.

Sitting on my new speckled neon bedspread that resembled a '90s school picture-day backdrop, I pressed "TALK" on the cordless phone to call Caitlin or Katie or Kate or Erica or whoever answered me first. We had nothing to talk about but that wasn't the point. I was fourteen and that's what fourteen-year-olds did. Well, that's what fourteen-year-old girls did. I had all of their home phone numbers memorized and put my finger to the keypad to dial but there wasn't a dial tone.

"Did somebody just pick up the phone?" Mom asked. "Whoever you are please hang up the phoo-ooone. Spit spot."

I pressed the # key on the cordless to pretend I'd hung up and covered the receiver with my palm to block the wisps of my breathing. I'd mastered my eavesdropping skills years before. We all had. Living in a house with seven people and one phone line gave us lots of opportunities to practice.

"Sorry, Mom," Mom said to my Grandmother Lenore. "It's just us again."

"That's all right, Deb."

"So what do you think I should do? Because I gotta tell you, I'm at a total loss."

Oo, this is a good one, I thought.

"Well, hun, for starters don't lose hope."

"Might be a little late for that, Mom. I think she's slipped too far this last year already and I'm not sure how to get her back. Remember how as a little girl she would only wear dresses? I tried explaining to her that first year what winter meant and that she'd need some jeans to walk through two feet of snow. And still when the snow fell she would only wear dresses."

"I'm not a fan of seeing Michelle's boxers peeking out from her baggy pants either, but you can't get so worked up over fashion."

"It's not just the outfits. It's that she wants to paint her room black. It's her drinking and smoking and sex and sneaking out at night and lying about all of it and probably more. It's like she's stopped caring and I don't know why."

"She's a teenager. No point wondering why she does what she does. Do I need to remind you what you were like when you were 13?"

"No, please don't. I remember it all on my own. But there's something more here. I sense it in her. I just wish I knew what it was."

"Do you?"

"Yeah. I think she needs me to know."

"How are the other kids?"

I shifted in bed, listening closer than before.

"Oh yes—then there's them. My other four children. You know, I try to give them attention too but most of my energy right now is aimed at Michelle. And Jim's around but I'm the one who's dealing with it."

"But he and Michelle are so close."

"Were."

"Really?"

"She used to be able to make him laugh. Even during all his drama at work a couple years ago she knew just what to say to get him out of the funk that's been growing in him. Now it's not the same. I haven't heard him laugh—like really laugh—in months."

"I'm sorry, sweetheart."

"It will get better. I'm sure it will. Can't get worse, right?"

"You've gotten this far, kiddo."

"Yes we have. And we're going to keep it up. Jim and I agreed that whoever applies for a divorce first gets custody of the kids and I know that's not gonna be me."

"I guess that's one way to keep a marriage going."

"Hey, a mother's gotta do what a mother's gotta do."

"Yes, well a grandmother does, too. I was thinking . . . you know the money from Daddy's life insurance?"

"Oh no. Mom, I haven't even asked how you're coping. There is just so much with work and this and . . ."

"We need a family vacation. Maybe that will reset things back to normal. Your father died 30 years before he was supposed to, so we need to live his retirement for him."

"I'm at the point that I'll try anything. Where do you want to go?"

"How about Disney World?"

No way! The farthest vacation we'd dared take in ten years was to the Mall of America. I bounced on my bed and the springs squeaked.

"Who's on the phone? Get off the phoooo-oone!"

~

Meredith squealed all the way down the Hollywood Tower of Terror. A teenager dressed as a bellhop in red had buckled her into the safety seat between Michelle and me. We had stood in line for nearly an hour to get to the top of the amusement ride so we could plummet to the bottom in less than three seconds.

"I'm going to fly away!" she screamed as the elevator dropped 100 feet. While my weightless bladder made nice with my lungs, Meredith's skinny legs rose through the waist bar. Her black hair was standing straight up in the air—not from fright but physics. I pushed her back down on the seat, trying to make up for her lost inertia with my little strength.

My glasses were slipping off my nose so I let go of Meredith to nudge them up. Her waist bar rattled and her body began to levitate again. I reached back over and held her down until the elevator landed on the ground floor. On the other side of Meredith, Michelle held on to her own bar and endured the terror without sound or expression. She only gasped for air when the elevator changed directions and caught her off guard. The ride gave her no joy and Meredith's peril caused her no alarm.

"Mom, I didn't pee!" were the first words Meredith said when she ran out to Mom, who was waiting for us at the bottom by the exit with Jamie in her stroller. The Florida sun was Mom's worst enemy so she had parked under the shade of a shrub trimmed in the shape of a tutu-clad hippopotamus. Jamie licked a blue, yellow, and white ice cream bar that once upon a time may have been Donald Duck but had melted into an unrecognizable blob.

"You're so brave," Mom said and picked Meredith up in one arm.

"Goodness, that was fun," Grandmother Lenore said, fixing her stray silver hairs.

All eight of us fit inside the tiny boat that transported us through the *It's a Small World* ride. The moat water was dyed blue and smelled more like mechanics and mop buckets than magic. Yet we still circled the small world of glimmering stereotypes four times. Robotic ladies in saris danced in time to the flapping of an

Indian elephant's ears to the song written to benefit UNICEF back in the 1960s at the New York World's Fair when the world still had World's Fairs.

"Look Jordan, there's the Taj Mahal," Mom pointed at the plaster stage the first time we rode around the small world.

"Is that like the real one in India?"

"Jim, you've been to the real one. How do these two compare?"

"This one's more retro. I don't believe India had glitter or spray paint in 1632. But yes, I can see the similarities."

"It's beautiful. Right, Michelle? So, so beautiful."

"Whatever, Jordan."

"Michelle, can you believe we're in Disney World? You and me are in Disney World!"

"You don't have to tell me where I am, Jordan."

"But you're in Disney World!"

"Yeah. I know."

"With Mickey Mouse and rides and Aladdin and sun and Mom and Dad and Grandma and . . ."

"Be quiet, Jordan."

"Look it! Look over there! It's a leprechaun!"

By the fourth time Mom stepped off the boat and onto the loading dock at the end of the ride, she had to hold extra firmly to the railing. "OK kids, I feel queasy. That's enough small world voyaging for me."

"Please, Mom! One more, one more time pretty please?" Meredith chirped, still in the boat and not about to get out without a struggle.

"If I want to see what kids from all around the world look like, I don't need to get seasick watching animatronic dolls. Now get out of the boat."

"It's not really a boat, Mom," I told her. "It's on a track. Like a train."

"I am aware of that, White Boy."

"Yeah, Aaron. You know, Mom's not a potted plant." Not a day went by when Mom didn't tell us she was "not a potted plant." And she informed Jordan of the fact more than any of us. "You know that, Aaron?"

"Thank you, Jordan," Mom said.

"Where's Michelle?" Dad asked.

"She's up there." Meredith pointed. "I'll go get her!"

"Get back here, Meredith!"

Meredith was already running to the top of the cement ramp and Jordan chased behind her. "Jordan! Meredith—Bus!"

All the white all-American families who were calmly walking toward the exit leapt aside to stand as close as they could to the handrails as two little brown savages sprinted through the middle of the path like a pair of "it's a small world" robots on the run.

Later, I stood outside our hotel with Mom as she finished a cigarette before bed. She had quit smoking when she became pregnant with me and had been nicotine free ever since except for the occasional hit of Nicorette gum if she'd had a tense day. She had started smoking again full time a year before when her days of the week were no longer categorized as *tense* or *not tense* but instead were sorted as *just mildly maddening* or *worthy of eating a gun.*

"Make sure Michelle stays in the hotel tonight, alright?"

"Where would she go, Mom?"

"I don't know. Orlando's not all princess castles and fairy tales."

"OK, but why would she go?"

"Don't know that either." She took a drag on her cigarette and blew the smoke upward, ruffling her blonde bangs. "I still haven't been able to figure that part out yet."

I bent my neck back to see the four-story pineapple jutting out the side of our hotel like a colossal pop-up book about tropical fruits. It was yellow and glowed bright in the rays of three spotlights that also shone into the rooms on that side of the hotel.

"Will she get better you think?" I asked.

"Maybe she'll get better. Maybe worse. I asked her the other day how she would feel about being a prostitute to make a living. Because I gotta say, that's the path I see her walking right now." Mom had no idea at the time that it was a path Michelle was already all too familiar with.

"Oh."

"Sorry, big guy. I know this is tough on you."

"It's OK. Things are OK."

"She's your best friend."

"Yeah."

"So it's OK if it's tough on you." Mom snuffed out the nub of her cigarette on the pavement with the toe of her white Reeboks while reaching in her pocket for her lighter. "Maybe one more."

"I'm OK, Mom. Everything's OK."

She took her first draw, which she always held the longest. "Do you ever blame your dad and me?"

"For what?"

"For changing your life. It used to be so good."

"Uhm, I'm at Disney World. Life's pretty good."

"It could have been better. You've given up a lot."

"I got a lot, too."

"You could have done everything. Had everything."

"Why are we talking about this?"

"You're so innocent that's all."

"Is that bad?"

"I can't tell."

"Oh."

"Just promise me you won't let Michelle leave the hotel."

Michelle stayed in the hotel all night. We slept on the pullout sofa bed together head to toe. The hotel phone rang at 5:00 AM.

I answered. "Hello."

"Good morning, ma'am. Wake up call."

"Thanks," I said, not bothering to correct my gender to the concierge. I was used to it. Every time a telemarketer phoned our house selling knives or polling our opinions about President Clinton's infidelity, they would ask me if they could speak to my husband. "I'm a single Mom," I'd tell them. "And I have to get my kids their supper now."

"Oh, I'm very sorry, Madame. It said here in our files . . ." they'd say before I hung up on them.

At the Pineapple Inn, Mom and Dad moved about in the other room getting Jamie and Meredith dressed. Grandmother was in charge of Jordan.

"Wake up, Michelle."

She rolled over.

"Time to go home."

"Fine." She sat up, slipped on her shoes, and crossed her arms staring at the cartoon-goldfish-themed border pasted along the line of the room's ceiling. The bottom cusp of the wallpaper was loose and curled. One of the fish was wearing a monocle that had been scribbled onto his left eye with a blue pen by a previous guest. Michelle had commented on the graffiti when we first checked in. Now as we checked out, I followed her eyes and looked up at the wallpaper. The bespectacled goldfish now had X's in his eyes.

"Why'd you do that?" I asked.

"Whatever. Let's go."

"Aren't you going to brush your teeth?"

"Nah."

"But you always do. You have the whitest teeth."

"I don't feel like it."

We sat by each other and a stranger on the plane back to Nebraska. Michelle had brought a deck of cards and the two of us played a mindless game of War on the flip-down tray tables for three hours until the plane started to descend. Then in a patch of turbulence our descent went into overdrive, and we plummeted 1,000 feet in one second.

"Woo-weee!" I heard Grandmother Lenore squeal from a few rows up ahead through my clogged eardrums.

The plane jolted upward. Then shot back down.

"Now I really am going to pee my pants!" Meredith screamed.

"At least your seatbelt fits this time, right?" Dad asked.

I would have chosen wetting my pants over what happened next. The airplane's jerky up-and-down was shaking me up like a Coke bottle. When the spicy stomach acid touched my esophagus I reached for the *SkyMall* magazine in the seatback in front of me and opened it up to a random page before hurling all over its display of precise portion pet feeders. Like yawning, vomiting had always been contagious for Michelle. So while I was mid-heave, she leaned forward alongside me and let her guts go. She didn't have enough warning time to grab her own *SkyMall*, however, so I shared mine. When we were both empty, we closed the magazine gently to not splash and slid it under my chair. Then we had a giggle fit until the plane was on the ground as we tried to avoid making eye contact with the man beside us in the aisle seat who plugged his nose to block our stench.

"Goodness, me! I didn't know we were going to have any more thrill rides on this vacation," Grandmother Lenore said when we collected each other in the terminal. "Hey," she paused to inhale. "What's that smell?"

"Yeah. What is that smell?" Mom asked.

"It smells like the car trip to Uncle David's house in Chicago," Dad said. "When everyone got the stomach flu and threw up all the way through Iowa."

"That's us," I said.

"Really? You too, Michelle?"

"Aaron started it."

She and I laughed again while the rest of our family backed away for fresh air. It was the last time we would laugh together for years.

ONCE WE RETURNED FROM Disney World, I gradually began to know all about Michelle's plunge into emotional darkness. I didn't even have to eavesdrop on the telephone anymore to find out about it. Now my family talked about it—fought about it—out in the open.

I knew she was seeing a therapist but it wasn't working because she wouldn't speak during the sessions. I knew why she added make-up to her swollen cheek after an older girl beat her up for cheating with her boyfriend. I knew that Mom and Dad installed a security system not to keep burglars out of our house but to keep Michelle in at night. I knew that she and I had run out of things to talk about after years of telling each other everything. I also knew we were an ordinary family and life would be back to normal soon. Soon I'd find out I didn't know shit.

"Your sister is trying to kill herself in the basement," Mom said. It was 10:58 PM and I'd barely made my curfew and closed the door to the garage of our new house. Mom and Dad were originally looking to buy a different six-bedroom house on Water Tower Court when they noticed a "For Sale" sign across the street. The house looked like a cathedral on the outside, and when they pressed their faces to the glass windows, they saw a Maharajan palace on the inside. Indian ogee archways divided the rooms and wooden balconies overlooked them. No other place in Nebraska was so custom made for our family so we bought it, sold the pink house, and moved into the mogul mansion with a three-car garage. The first thing I remember when I came in from that garage on that night that I don't like remembering was Mom sitting on a chair in the kitchen. She clutched a can of Diet Coke as she waited for me to get home.

"You're the only one who can save her," she said.

"Fffuuuck You!" Michelle's voice trembled through the air vent downstairs.

"Dad's down there." Mom took a pull from the aluminum can.

"What's happening?"

"Don't you hear that? She's going psychotic. You are the only one who can save her."

"Yeah, you said that. But what am I supposed to do?"

"Save her."

"OK, but . . . but how?"

"Fuuucckkk!!"

"Be her brother. I can't be her mother right now. I know I'm supposed to but I can't. I'm so sorry, White Boy. I can't. I really can't."

"You don't even look upset." My eyes were filming with tears that tilted my contact lenses so the world looked crooked.

"Too upset to look like it, I guess."

"Where's everybody else?"

"Cried themselves to sleep upstairs already."

"So now I have to go downstairs?"

"Yes. Talk to your sister."

The carpet on the stairs down to the basement was sapphire. I picked at its threads as I sat on the top step, delaying my duty. I was beginning to feel more at ease when I heard more of Michelle's outbursts at Dad. Like a thunderstorm, her screams of "Fuck You! Fffuucckkk Yoooouuu! Fuck you fuck you fuck you fuck you!!!!" started losing some of their shock after the twentieth strike. Her panting in between each tantrum, however, lit me with a fresh fear every time. I hadn't heard that noise since her fits her first summer when Mom forced her to turn off *I Love Lucy* and come to dinner. It sounded like a demon was trapped in her chest and was straining to get out.

I slid down the steps one by one on my butt, dreading the moment when I would land at the bottom. Then I crawled to her door and counted off the intervals between her eruptions, waiting for 30 seconds of calm before making my entrance. When 35 . . . 36 . . . 37 ticked off in my mind, I wiped my eyes, stood up, and stepped inside her bedroom.

"Hi Michelle."

She was on the ground. Her face was glossy with tears and snot and slobber that she couldn't wipe away because Dad was holding down her wrists to the carpet. Looking around the destroyed room I assumed he'd cuffed her hands with his so she couldn't throw anything else at him.

"Fffffffffffffffuuuuuuuuuckk!"

"Nice to see you, too," I said.

Michelle whimpered.

"What do you want? A tissue? You need it. Your face is a mess."

"Get Dad aawwwaaaay from me!"

"No, Michelle. You don't fucking get it," Dad said, tensing his grip as she struggled to escape. "You don't get to do this to us. To yourself."

As she slumped forward her black hair covered her and Dad's hands. Then, possessed, she sprang up and set herself loose and started clawing at Dad. "Fuck fuck fuck fuck fuck fuck you! Fuck you!" Twice her weight, he fought back until Michelle was subdued and curled up on the ground once more.

"Dad!" I yelled. "Stop, Dad."

He stopped and let go.

"I got it, Dad."

"OK." He left her room and walked up the sapphire staircase to sanctuary.

Left alone with me, Michelle cowered in one corner and leaned against her black bookshelf. The top shelf displayed the porcelain doll collection that she'd started on her first birthday in America. The bottom shelf was where she hid the bottles of vodka she liked to mix with Mountain Dew. I cowered in the other corner of the room, stared at her, and tried to recognize the girl ten feet away from me. She was sedated. Exhausted from hours of screaming.

"What's wrong?"

"I just want to die."

"No you don't!"

"I do. It's all I want."

"Don't say that to me."

"You don't know what it's like. How I feel."

"No obviously not since I'm not the one going crazy."

"I'm not crazy."

"Then what are you? Because let me tell you, you're acting crazy."

"What I feel feels right. It doesn't feel crazy. I . . . *sigh* . . . I feel like dying."

"Stop saying that."

"I don't want to do this anymore."

"Promise you'll stop saying that."

Silence.

"Promise!" I crab-walked on my hands and feet to her corner. "Pinky-swear me." I held out my right hand and extended my pinky. She looped her finger around mine.

"Let's watch *Clueless?*" I asked, desperate to do something besides talk about suicide.

We lay beneath blankets on the couch as we watched *our* movie three times in a row on the television outside her bedroom. Michelle fell asleep midway through the second viewing but as soon as it finished, I rewound the tape and started over. I still knew every line but watched it anyway. I wasn't going to sleep until the sun was up again and she had survived the night.

Two months later Mom went downstairs to wake Michelle up for school. She was sick in bed. An empty bottle of Prozac without its cap was on the ground beside a can of Mountain Dew.

"Michelle, were you trying to commit suicide?"

"Yes."

"Get up. We're going to the hospital," Mom said stoically. She tried to find the strength to be Michelle's mother, but to succeed she had to part from her emotions, treat the situation like her job, and address Michelle's immediate needs. "We've gotta pump your stomach and get out the poison."

The rest of the family was in the dining room eating cereal for breakfast when Mom lugged Michelle past us and opened the garage door. Dad understood what was happening in an instant and stood up to carry her the rest of the way outside.

"Thanks, Jim. OK everybody in the van," Mom said. "Spoons down. We have to go to the hospital. Michelle's sick."

The ride was silent. When Dad pulled the van in front of the psych ward sign instead of the emergency room, Michelle knew something was up. We'd been to this hospital hundreds of times by now and knew every turn in the parking lot. Michelle summoned all her energy and went ballistic in the seat next to me. She kicked the back of Dad's driver's seat and lunged over me to open the door and flee.

"Aaron, don't let your sister get away," Dad instructed.

"Fuuuuck youu!" she cried as I forcefully held her down.

I wanted to look out the car window like I always had and pretend everything was okay, but that was no longer an option. When Michelle lost her sanity, I finally lost my innocence and let go of my illusions about my family. We could have as many plastic deer, basketball hoops, ferns, and minivans in our front yard as all the other households on the street but we would never be like them and we never had been. We were different, and there were no surgeries or routines or Disney vacations that could normalize us. After living a fantasy for so many years, I finally saw what we were, and my family no longer felt familiar to me.

Michelle struggled all the way to the admitting desk of the psych unit. As Mom and Dad filled out the paperwork to make her a ward of the state of Nebraska, a pair of nurses in teal dragged her down the white tile hallway as she screamed back at us, "You lied! You said you'd never leave me! Don't leave me! Please! Please don't leave."

Then we left.

Chapter Ten

A GLOBAL FAMILY CHRISTMAS

In a game of Global Family Bingo, my parents' playing card still has a few empty spaces. The most notable blank is Africa. "All our Christmas photo needs now is an Africa baby," Mom says each December to Dad even though she's really talking to all her children gathered around the tree. "I'm not going to have any more kids, but Jim, wouldn't you love an African grandbaby?"

"Yes, dear."

"You kids all hear that? Now don't misunderstand. I don't want to hear about any of you getting knocked up—at least not yet."

"OK, Mom."

"You're all too young still."

"Yeah, I'm only 13." Jamie threw her hands up, knocking a silver ornament off the tree. "Sheesh."

"But when you're ready to adopt from Africa, you just tell me the good news and you'll have your father's and my full support."

"OK, Mom. We'll get back to you in 20 years. Will you take the picture now?"

We roll our eyes at her, but the odds of one of us adopting from a sub-Saharan African country are rising. Asian countries like China (whose one-child policy led to an alarming number of abandoned girls) and South Korea (the country that started it all) led the world in international adoption for the last two decades but now they are starting to shy away from sending their babies to other countries as a solution to their persistent orphan problem. They feel ashamed that, although they have strong economies and skyscrapers and an Olympic Games opening ceremony that made the world pee its pants a little, they can't take care of their children. So they're limiting the number of children they allow to be internationally adopted each year.

I found that my siblings' homelands have flourished since they've been gone. The cycle of international adoption is nearly complete in India and Korea and soon domestic adoptions will reign. That's fantastic news for the hundreds of thousands of children living there, but it's left me feeling like I was missing something on my journey. After visiting the countries where my siblings got their start, I had a strong sense of their history and their heritage. Yet I failed to completely grasp the gravity of their situation. I didn't get to know what it was like for them in an era when abandoning the country was their only hope of a home.

Confronted with the orphans' despair, Thomas Coram opened the Foundling Hospital in eighteenth-century London. Charles Loring Brace bought train tickets for thousands of street urchins in nineteenth-century Manhattan. The Holts flew around the world and brought home eight babies of a different race from twentieth-century Korea. To get a true sense of what had motivated them and to complete my quest, I needed to visit the twenty-first-century equivalent of these historical places. So I traveled to Ethiopia, international adoption's next frontier, for Christmas.

Gross National Income per capita in terms of Purchasing Power Parity dollars sounds like the invention of some narcissistic economist. But basically, a country's GNI per capita in PPP is the average amount of money a person in that country makes in a year in relation to how much it costs to live in that country compared to other countries. So it can tell a lot about what life is like for a country's people. According to the World Bank, in 2008 Ethiopia's GNI per capita in PPP was $870 while that of the United States was $48,430. Ethiopia is not only one of the poorest nations in the world, it is almost the poorest nation in Africa. Geographically, it is the hole of a poisonous donut, surrounded by genocidal Sudan, refugee-flooded Uganda, politically flammable Kenya, hostile Eritrea, and swashbuckling Somalia. Ethiopia's dark history of famine—the country's main claim to fame—is now being eclipsed by AIDS. The population is overgrown at 83 million, of which an estimated 6 million children are orphans.

Despite the poverty, I found that beauty breaks through the heartache in Ethiopia. Friends greet each other on the unlabeled dirt city street with twenty kisses on the cheek. These aren't "Oh Daaaaaahling, you look fabulous, love your Prada" kisses. They're rich. They have soul.

It's this soul at Christmastime in Ethiopia that led me to find what I was truly missing. I had gone looking for poverty, and I found it in sick amounts. Yet I never expected that it would be Ethiopia's riches that would help me relate and reunite with my siblings for good.

My parents celebrated Valentine's Day each year with a 16-piece bucket of Popeyes Fried Chicken. It was the only place in town without a wait. Their restaurant choice was not really surprising when you consider this was the same couple that got married on January 1 for tax purposes. They could have said they chose the date because it represented a new beginning or they thought the sight of their clouds of cold breath in the winter Nebraska air was romantic. But nope. They just wanted the bigger tax break.

Ever since their wedding day set the precedent, all of our family holidays have been a little off. Traditional traditions simply weren't our style. We never lit fireworks on the Fourth of July. Mom and Dad were too afraid that one of us kids would light our front lawn on fire in the process and then the neighbors would finally have proof that we were pagans. Instead we bought red, white, and blue streamers and a jumbo bag of glow sticks to drape on our bikes and three-wheelers. As the five of us rode back and forth on the street after sunset, we left behind patriotic streaks in the darkness.

We also celebrated more holidays than any other family on the block—and I'm not even counting the cultural Indian and Korean ones we were forced to endure. I've lost count of the number of sitar concerts I've attended or the number of kimchi dinners I've eaten that burned my tongue. In addition to all of those proud heritage moments, each of my siblings also had an anniversary of their homecoming day. They opened presents, and we ate cake and watched the video of their airport arrival for the umpteenth time.

The only holiday of ours that resembled most everyone else's in America was Easter. We boiled eggs, dyed eggs, hid eggs, found eggs, and then ate eggs like most Easter-celebrating families in the country. Not my friend Legs' family though. In Mumbai, after Legs pierced her nose on the wet street, we returned to our hotel room overlooking the hospital. Legs confessed to me the truth of her childhood Easters growing up in a capital-C Catholic family. After the church service, her family invited their priest over to their house for dinner theater. As he ate ham at the dining table, Legs and her siblings reenacted the Passion of the Christ. Legs's littlest brother played Jesus because he was the only who was young enough to tolerate being stripped down to his tighty whiteys to be paraded around the living room with a homemade wooden cross strapped to his back.

"Who were you playing then in this charade?" I asked Legs.

"One of the weeping women."

"In front of your priest?"

"Hell yes!"

"You have got to be kidding me . . ."

We had our own pageant once but it was on Christmas Eve when you are supposed to have pageants. The venue was the chapel at Eastmont Towers Retirement Community where Grandmother Lenore and orphan-train rider Ann Mabel Harrison lived. I played the upright piano, Meredith led the songs, and Jordan lit the candles for the forty residents who came down from their rooms for some holiday cheer. Jamie, who was three, helped turn the pages to *The Polar Express* that Meredith read while I tinkled out *'Twas the Night before Christmas* on keyboard in the background.

Michelle wasn't anybody in our family pageant. Not Mary, a wisewoman, or a donkey. She was institutionalized in a home for troubled girls in Omaha that year. Her stay in the insanity wing of the hospital only lasted until Mom and Dad were able to get her a bed at the Uta Halee psychiatric residence in Omaha, an hour's drive away from our house in Lincoln. While living at Uta Halee, which translates to "on the sunny side" in the Omaha tribe's language, Michelle went to group therapy sessions, one-on-one therapy sessions, family therapy sessions, and school lessons all within the lockdown facility.

On the day of our Christmas Eve pageant, Michelle was only six months into her treatment, but I hadn't seen her in three. At first the whole family had spent Sunday afternoons driving up to visit her. We had parked outside the stone building and walked into the basement recreation room where she'd been waiting for us, angrily. Then all seven of us sat around a foldable card table and tried to put together an oversized jigsaw puzzle. The fifteen families around us all did the same. Without much speaking we rushed to finish the puzzle, frantic to find the missing pieces so we could go home and away from the awkward but unexplained evidence of our family's dysfunction. Then three months into her therapy sessions, Michelle had let out the reason for her meltdown. She confessed the dark secret she had been hiding from the police in India, her caretakers at the BSSK orphanage, and our mom and dad. But instead of reconstructing the broken pieces of my family's normalcy, the news had made the edges all the more jagged.

"And then she made me have sex with the man," Michelle said she told her therapist, three months into their sessions together.

"Who made you, Michelle?"

"My mom . . . my Indian mom."

"To get your brother back, your mother forced you to have sex with his kidnapper?"

"Yeah."

"How old were you?"

"Really little. Five maybe."

"Did it ever happen again?"

"Yeah."

"Did it happen again a lot?"

"Yeah."

"I am so sorry, Michelle. No one should have done that to you."

"Maybe."

"No. No one should have hurt you. How did you feel?"

"I don't know."

"How did you feel, Michelle?"

"Guilty, I guess."

"Do you still feel guilty?"

"Yes."

"Is that why you feel like punishing yourself?"

"Yes."

Mom vomited when she found out the past her daughter had kept locked away from all of us for ten years. After the truth was revealed, Mom and Dad were the only family members who were allowed to visit Michelle. It was just too difficult for Michelle to recover with all of us around picking at the scabs of her past, so we stayed home on Sundays while Michelle and Mom and Dad sat in the rec room trying to put the puzzle together on their own. Even though the therapist thought the rest of us would aggravate Michelle's post-traumatic stress disorder, we were given special permission on Christmas Eve to visit. Everybody thought it would be good to maintain some of the family traditions. So after our Eske Family Christmas Pageant, we got in the car and drove to Omaha to try and eat dinner together as one big happy family once more.

On past Christmas Eves we had piled the whole family, grandmothers and all, into a van and gone to the candlelight service at First Plymouth Church, the first church we'd been to when Michelle and Jordan came home. We still sat in the balcony. The best view on Christmas Eve was from up there anyway.

Every year, as the choir sang "Silent Night," the lights dimmed to darkness and everyone in the congregation took out the white candles the usher had handed us before the service began. An acolyte in a white robe touched his wick to the Advent candle burning on the front altar and then he passed the flame on to the overeager churchgoers sitting in the first row. Candle to candle, the flame was extended to all. By the second stanza of the song, the light had spread through most of the sanctuary below. It wouldn't reach us up in the balcony until the final chorus. In the meantime, Michelle and I leaned forward over the ledge, taking in the calm bright view and reflecting because that's what you do at Christmas.

After the church service, we all smooshed back into the van and drove through town to see the luminaries that lined the streets like flares at the scene of a car accident. Entire neighborhoods set out thousands of these white paper lunch bags with candles glowing inside like an angelic jack-o-lantern. Mannheim Steamroller's synthesizer Christmas albums played from the car speakers. Grandmother Lenore sang along by herself to the songs she knew.

When we had driven along almost every street in Lincoln, we returned home to continue our holiday traditions. The house smelled like chili powder that simmered in the crock-pot on the kitchen counter. Soon the scent of cinnamon would overpower the chili. We ate chili and cinnamon rolls every Christmas Eve. Dipping oozy white icing in a bowl of beans may not sound very orthodox, but it was our tradition.

I CARRIED ON THE CHILI TRADITION as best I could while eating Christmas Eve dinner alone in a Chinese restaurant in Ethiopia's capital city, Addis Ababa.

"Fried kidney beans and rice?" I ordered, pointing at the trilingual menu in the candlelight.

"Ishee," the Ethiopian waitress replied. The word *ishee* was the only word in the Ethiopian Amharic language I needed to know. It could mean OK, cool, thanks, hello, or whatever you wanted it to mean from what I could tell. It was a linguistic chameleon. A very smurfy word.

"Ishee," I said and handed my menu back to the waitress who was wearing a hot red silk *qípáo.* She walked away gracefully in the Chinese garment.

The power in this city of 3 million people was out. Again. The back-up generator at the orphanage I was visiting had been working overtime all week to keep the lights on for the kids. In the China Resta Urant, a few dozen skinny white candles stuffed in the necks of used Chinese-labeled liquor bottles melted slowly. They lit the little room in the absence of the hundreds of electric lanterns that hung unlit from the ceiling like sleeping bats in a low cave. A jungle of red and green Christmas garlands ran through the paper lanterns like shimmering vines. Silver bells bordered the blank television set.

I sat by myself at a table for two. Two Ethiopian men ate Mongolian beef with their fingers in the corner. Beside me, a large Chinese family spun a loaded lazy Susan round and round, occasionally halting to feed a loitering Ethiopian 3-year-old a piece of fried squirrelfish. The child's father looked on, unconcerned.

"What's up, dude?" A third man pulled a chair up to the guys' table in the corner with a doctored American swagger and shoveled a wad of Mongolian beef into his hand like popcorn.

"Ishee."

My fried kidney beans arrived and turned out to be green beans. They weren't the traditional Eske chili knockoff I was hoping for, but I was a little relieved nonetheless not to be eating a bowl of kidney beans all alone. "Thanks, ahmasaygunalo," I said. The oily green beans slipped through my disposable chopsticks and I started eating them like French fries with my fingers.

There was a sudden flurry of Mandarin voices, and I looked over, expecting to see the Chinese family grimacing from their fifth Christmas shot of *baijiu* alcohol. Instead, they were all looking at the Ethiopian 3-year-old whose jaw was mutely open while his fingers froze stiff and extended. A piece of squirrelfish was lodged in his throat.

A dual clock above the doorway told the time in Addis and Beijing. 7:27 PM, 12:27 AM. The Chinese father stood. The Ethiopian child's father rushed over. He turned his son's face toward the candlelight and started fishing in his mouth for the unchewed chunk. No luck. Then he and the Chinese father began pounding the kid's back. Bruising pounds.

"Hug him hard!" I said and the Amharic and Mandarin voices hushed to hear my foreign language. "Hug him," I repeated, fisting up my lower ribcage from my chair. The father began pumping his son's sternum from behind. All I could hear was the dad's rapid breathing as he trusted the advice of the white *firangi* foreigner punching himself in the gut. The "hey dude" trio in the corner looked inward at what was left of their Mongolian beef, too scared to witness a choking. The lazy Susan was still. The red-dressed waitress stood like a statue, holding a water pitcher with her left hand and covering her agape mouth with her right. The Chinese father crouched and patted the Ethiopian father's back. The man was softly pleading with his son in a language I had never heard but that we all understood.

A few thrusts later and the child gave a croak. A white-pink lump rolled onto the linoleum floor in a pool of stomach juice.

As I stood and counted my Ethiopian *birr* to pay for dinner, the power came on. The lanterns three inches above me lit my hair an electric red. A Christmas tree I hadn't noticed in the dark came ablaze in fat colorful bulbs, gold stars, and snowman ornaments. A two-week-old soccer game between Chelsea and Arsenal repeated on the formerly blank television. The waitress pressed "play" on the boom box and Mariah Carey began to belt about all she wanted for Christmas. It was our favorite—Michelle's and mine. Of course it was everybody's favorite but it was especially ours.

THE RADIO STATION PLAYED Mariah's "All I Want for Christmas Is You" twice on our drive from Lincoln to Omaha to see Michelle on

Christmas Eve afternoon. We hadn't bothered to change out of the dress clothes we'd worn in the Christmas pageant. We wanted to get to be with our lost sister as quickly as possible.

"You all stay here," Dad said when he parked at Uta Halee. "I'll go check her out and we'll be back."

Michelle was wearing a droopy sweatshirt when she emerged from the lockdown building that had been designed to look as much like a house as possible. Her unbrushed hair was tied back in a ponytail. The handles of a shopping sack hung on the crook of her arm. I opened the sliding door of the minivan for her and she shuffled over my legs and sat in the empty seat next to mine.

"Hi," I said.

"Hmm," she replied and sneered at me. She didn't need to waste any more syllables for me to interpret her meaning. It was the same greeting she'd given me in the puzzle room months before. It was her way of grumbling, "If you hadn't strapped me down in the car outside the hospital, I could have made a run for it and never ended up locked in a home for psychos where everyone else is crazier than I am and I'm only allowed to leave for forced Christmas Eve dinners with my family who are a bunch of traitors."

"Merry Christmas," I said although the rise in my tone at the end sounded more like a question.

"Yep," she said.

"Michelle, we were thinking of eating at this Arabic restaurant downtown," Mom interjected. "You know, something different than usual. Plus we called ahead and it's open and nowhere else is. How's that sound?"

"Fine."

"OK, then."

"How was school this week?" Dad asked.

"Stupid. Everyone's so stupid."

"Do you get a Christmas break?" Grandmother Lenore asked from the back of the van.

"Yep."

"How many days?"

"Doesn't really matter does it? Every day is awful. Go to school. Don't go to school. It's always going to be bad."

"Oh, I don't like the sound of that."

"Me neither, Grandma. I could come back to Lincoln and be with my friends and it would be better."

"That's not an option, Schmellie," Mom said in the passenger seat. "Sorry."

"But that's where I'd be happy."

"You weren't happy before, were you?"

"Not with you guys. With my friends."

"We love you, Michelle."

"If you say so, Mom."

"Jamie, do you love your sister Michelle?"

"Yeeees."

"See, we love you."

"Then why do you make me stay here?"

"So you can get better."

"That's not going to happen."

"Let me tell you something, Michelle. I promised myself this morning I wouldn't say this, but this sucks for me, too. You know, this isn't exactly my Christmas wish come true."

"So why are you here? Why not leave me again?"

"Because we're going to do all we can to help you be healthy again. So no more attitude. Please."

"Fine."

We were one of a handful of cars on the road as we drove into downtown Omaha toward the city's one-and-a-half skyscrapers. The second tower's cornerstone had been laid earlier in the year, and we could still see through its 634-foot steel skeleton. The limbs of the trees that were spaced out evenly to fit four to a city block were bare as well. Dad parallel parked and plugged the meter for ninety minutes with three quarters even though he was probably hoping he'd only get his money's worth out of two of them.

The host placed us by the bathroom at the rear of the restaurant. I sat at the end of the table. During the first fifty-three minutes of dinner, the only words I spoke were, "I'll have the Aladdin Combo," "More water, please," "Jordan, will you quit tapping your foot already?" and "I didn't kick you that hard. Mom, I swear I didn't mean to kick him that hard."

The conversation all the way down the table was equally stilted. Grandmother Lenore tried a few more times to engage Michelle, but each exchange lasted about as long as a tennis volley between John McEnroe and a retired nun.

"So tell me about your friends," Grandmother served.

"I don't have any," Michelle spiked back.

Love–15.

"You have a nice big lawn up here. What's your room like?"

"It's ugly. There's not even a mirror."

"Why not?"

"They think I'm going to break it and cut myself with the shattered glass," Michelle shot across the table with topspin.

Love–30.

"But if I really wanted to slit my wrists I could just unscrew the light bulb in the ceiling and smash it onto the floor and pick up the shards. That would do it."

Love–40.

"Oh please, Michelle. Don't talk like that."

"Sorry, Grandma. I'm not saying I'm going to do that. It's just stupid I can't have a mirror. That's all."

15–40.

"Well you may not be able to see it for yourself right now but you look beautiful."

"I look like trash."

Game Michelle.

When the plates of Christmas kebabs and hummus arrived, we all stared down at them as we ate, relieved to have something else to look at awkwardly besides each other. In the absence of joyful chatter, Persian music pierced the air from the one big speaker anchored to the ceiling. A whining violin and wooden flute kept the beat for a woman who cried "Laaa murraa-eee-aan," to a man who cried back, "Soo-whoa-oo quaaa-ee-maaan" in high vibrato.

The waitress brought our bill before we had even finished eating. She must have sensed in our silence the desire to leave without lingering for coffee and dessert.

"Michelle, do you want to open your presents?" Mom asked.

"Actually, can I wait until tomorrow morning?"

"Why don't you just open them now?"

"I think I'm going to be a little lonely."

"Oh. Yes, wait then. I'm sorry, Michelle."

"Can't I just go home with you?" Her voice warbled. "It's all I want. To spend Christmas morning with my family."

"Not this year."

Michelle put her head down on the table. A chunk of her black hair floated in a bowl of baba ghanoush. Grandmother lifted the strands out with the fingers of her left hand while she rubbed Michelle's quaking back with her right.

Michelle sat back up, slouched, and wiped her tears and snot on the sleeve of her sweatshirt. "Fine," she said.

Driving away from the one-and-a-half city skyscrapers, Michelle gazed out her window in the back of the van. I pretended to gaze out the window too, but really I was looking at her and thinking of something nice to say. But nothing came to mind. I cleared my throat, hoping the momentum would trigger an idea. But twenty minutes later I'd only managed to say, "Mm," and had to finish that off with a fake "Mm-choo" because I had nothing more in my mind to say after "Michelle."

"Bless you, Aaron," Grandmother said.

Meredith and Jamie didn't stir from my fake sneeze. They were deep asleep with their heads on oversized pillows that, compared to their tiny bodies, could have been used as twin beds. Jordan read a scary story from a *Goosebumps* book, but he hadn't turned a page in miles. He—the boy whose mouth ran like a loose old muffler most days—had been the most silent of all during our visit. The van's engine worked harder to get up the hill to Uta Halee. Sensing that we were nearing the end, Michelle tugged under her seat and pulled out the shopping sack she'd shoved underneath when she first sat down. She dropped it on my lap.

"Sorry it isn't wrapped better," she said. "We're not allowed to have scissors either."

"Thanks, Michelle." I dipped my hand into the crumpled bag and felt the soft knit. It was a hand-knitted blue and white blanket. "Where did you get this? It's awesome."

"I made it in my spare time."

"You can knit?"

"I learned. It's for you to take to college next year."

"I will."

"Cool."

"I wish you could be with us tomorrow morning, too," I said even though I didn't wish that at all. After all those minutes looking at the back of her head blocking the window, I decided that lying was kinder than telling the truth. Earlier that morning while practicing the piano music one last time before the recital, I had never expected to feel this way around Michelle. Feel like getting her out of the car immediately and racing back to Lincoln to be alone. In the months when we'd been banned from each other I'd forgotten how uncomfortable we had grown when we were up close and impersonal. I wanted to be far, far away in a place where I could avoid facing the fact that my family no longer fit together.

IN JUNE 2003, AN ORPHAN named Ermias became a father to a boy named Dubella. A year later, malaria killed Ermias's wife, a heart problem killed him, and just like that, the son of an orphan became an orphan himself. For four years, little Dubella lived with his uncle's large family in Buge, a farming community in southern Ethiopia. A prolonged drought caused a food shortage, and Dubella's relatives, unable to care for him and all their other children, had to take him to the orphanage.

"Konjo, Dubella," I said at the top of the orphanage's stone staircase on Christmas morning in Addis. Dubella, now five, yanked the red hat down over his brown eyes when he spotted me. A baggy Santa suit concealed the rest of him except for a few fingertips poking out from the white arm cuffs and a gapped pair of permanent teeth biting his lower lip in a grin. I squatted and peeled back the cap to his half-grown eyebrows. "Merry Christmas, you."

The first morning I came to the orphanage, Dubella was drawing bumblebees. He sat cross-legged on the rug in the center of the room while smaller toddlers played around him. He was older than the oldest of the other children by two years. The age gap was emphasized by the hem of his daily overalls that stopped above his shin, exposing a few inches of leg. The straps on the overalls were stretched as long as they'd go. Most of the time only one strap was fastened anyway.

I sat beside Dubella. "Allo," I said and drew a purple turtle. He didn't speak, but replied by drawing a blue turtle on his sheet of paper. The week went on and we played tag and ball and he'd borrow my light-up Velcro watch until the alarm started to beep at four o'clock every day like a ticking grenade and he would want to get rid of it.

On this Christmas morning, I went digging inside a Santa suit that had been donated by some family in Michigan and found Dubella's hand buried inside. "Ready for the party?" I asked. "Let's go." I held his hand, and we went downstairs where twenty-five orphans dressed in traditional Ethiopian garb were gathered for an Americanized Christmas party. The girls wore ruffled yellow and pink dresses, and the boys wore traditional hand-embroidered white tunics. Everyone wore a cone birthday hat for Jesus. All the nurses and staff were there, even the ones off shift, to be a part of the day. When the chocolate birthday cake was gone, I sat beneath the star-topped plastic evergreen and watched the Christmas carnage as each child ripped open a present. I had experienced this scene many times before. Sheets of wrapping paper covered the floor. Some children squealed in joy as others looked on, jealous that they hadn't got the toy they wanted.

Dubella found my hiding spot under the plastic Christmas tree where I took in the mayhem of thirty Ethiopian orphans opening gifts. Dubella sat beside me and rested his tiny arm on my knee. I put mine around his shoulder. "Allo. What did Santa bring you from the North Pole, little Santa?"

Dubella picked up his present from the floor to show me. It was a tiny red racecar.

ALMOST EVERY YEAR AFTER HE came into our family, Jordan got a racecar for Christmas. "It's a lace car, Michelle! A led lace car!" he said the first Christmas he was at home while holding the remote-controlled red car over his head. He had other presents under the six-foot plastic tree, but this was the only one that mattered. Ever since he'd learned to say the word in English, Jordan had wanted to be a "dliver." Fire truck driver, monster truck driver, pizza delivery driver, taxicab driver—it didn't matter which. He just wanted to drive and drive fast.

"You like it, Jordan?" Dad asked. "Come over here and let's put in some batteries."

Once the car was juiced up, Jordan raced it around the living room while the rest of us finished opening our presents. He drove it over the strewn wrapping paper and crashed it into Meredith, who was sitting on a baby blanket in the middle of the room playing with discarded bows. She giggled when the rubber wheels revved up against her skin.

Jordan's racecars became a part of the holiday tradition. Just as sure as there'd be a golden angel on top of the plastic Christmas tree keeping watch over the rest of the homemade ornaments, we knew there'd be a racecar parked below. "Santa" deviated one year from the standard and got Jordan a Nintendo 64, which of course would not have been complete without the Mario Kart racing game. Even though Mario was about to celebrate his twelfth birthday, this was my family's first Nintendo. Regardless of the heat advisory or wind chill, Mom and Dad wanted us to be outside the house (while they remained inside) as many hours a day as possible. It was how they found brief moments of peace with the world. So they avoided buying any toys like Nintendos that might invite us to stay indoors.

The instant it was out of its wrapping, we all noticed Jordan's present. "Whoa, Jordan!" Michelle exclaimed and put down the box of makeup Mom and Dad had bought her in hopes she'd wear something on her face besides heavy black eyeliner. "You've been wanting that for so long." Meredith and I took a break from opening our own presents to join Jordan as he played with his. Jordan had all the Nintendo equipment plugged into the TV in less than a minute, as if he'd been imagining where to attach which cord for months. When it was all connected, we four oldest kids grabbed a controller while Jamie crawled in and out of the room to watch.

We chose our characters. Jordan picked Donkey Kong, Michelle wanted to be Princess Peach, and Meredith and I switched between a green dinosaur called Yoshi and some mushroom-like creature named Toad that every other kid on the block had known about for years except us.

For hours we chased each other around the cartoon racetrack.

"I got the power strip boost!"

"Quit littering your banana peels in front of me, Donkey."

"Then learn how to drive, Princess."

"How about you learn how to brush your teeth?"

"Jordan, did you not brush your teeth like I asked you to?" Mom said.

"This is awesome, Mom," Jordan said, crossing the finish line in first place for the fiftieth time and looking back at Mom. She sat on the couch behind us in a Santa sweatshirt that she and I had made during our one-on-one time two weeks before. Santa's beard was outlined in white puff-paint and the stars in the fabric night sky were daubed *periwinkle.* We made one together every year. Her dresser drawer had about as many puff-paint Christmas sweatshirts from years gone by as Jordan's toy chest had racecars.

"Glad you like it, Jordan. You're a pro driver. Don't forget to brush your teeth."

I finally crossed the finish line in last place.

"Let's go again!"

Grandmother sat down on the couch beside Mom. "You know, Deb, maybe you should have gotten them one of those play machines sooner."

"WHAT DID YOU GET, JORDAN?" Mom asked even though she already knew the answer. She had bought the gift and wrapped it weeks before, but she was trying to break the awkward silence around the tree. The mounds of presents under the evergreen were all there like usual. Mom was wearing a puff-paint *Grinch Who Stole Christmas* sweatshirt. Holiday tunes streamed from the boom box tuned to a radio station that had taken the day off from playing songs from Britney Spears's debut album to share the Christmas spirit with the fine Christian people of Lincoln. Everything was as it always was but not everyone was there. Michelle was back at Uta Halee, where we had left her the night before.

"It's a racecar," Jordan said. "Thanks."

He stood up, tossed the wrapping paper on the floor on top of the other scraps and carried his new car out of the room. After I'd finished opening my boxes stuffed with muscle-sized Abercrombie sweaters Mom wanted to believe would fit me, I searched the basement and the upstairs looking for Jordan. Then I peeked out the window and saw him driving the toy car in loops on the driveway. He was wearing a poofy black coat and stood in the center of the car's circles all by himself.

EVEN AFTER KNOWING ALL I KNOW and experiencing the side effects of adopting older children from other countries, I would still love to share every Christmas morning with a child like Dubella—my own adopted son like Dubella—and be the one of us to complete my family's bingo card. I probably can't, though. Not the way I'd want to. Most countries in the world today will not knowingly allow me to adopt, regardless of the laws in the States.

I was sixteen and Michelle was already at Uta Halee when I left my coming out letter in the book on Mom's nightstand—the philosophical *A Course in Miracles.* I couldn't summon the strength to tell Mom and Dad in person. Partly because I felt too disconnected to even bridge our relationships with words anymore. So I left the note in a place where I knew she would find it when she settled down to read. Then I went to a friend's house to spend the night and hide.

Today, when teenagers come out as gay, they *say* they're gay. When my peers and I did it in 2000, we *admitted* it. Being gay was just beginning to be accepted by the mainstream in America. Just two years earlier, Ellen Degeneres's television show about a lesbian bookstore owner was canceled, and a show about a gay Manhattan lawyer named Will and his redheaded roommate Grace was just about to begin. But the words "mainstream" and "Nebraska" never have belonged in the same sentence together.

The week before I told my parents that I was gay, there was a national election. Nebraska's ballots had a special box asking its citizens whether they wanted to ban same-sex marriage. Almost three out of four Nebraskans voted for the ban.

I returned home early Saturday morning, nervous to discover how Mom and Dad reacted to my letter. Well, I didn't wonder so much about what Mom would say. I figured she'd be fine. Most of her friends in college were gay guys. Most of her boyfriends turned out to be, too. But after years of Dad's building a wall of silent stoicism, I couldn't predict what would happen on my father's side. The words in my letter were the most intimate things I'd said to him in years—years in which the words "I love you" were not spoken. Raising five testing children and losing Michelle had created a distance between us demonstrated by how little we talked to each other. Overnight, my letter let out my secret and my feelings, and I was unsure how he would handle the outburst.

On my way to my room I passed Dad. Standing side by side in the hall, he didn't speak. He simply set his hand on my shoulder and held it there. One, two, three, four.

I CALLED DAD FROM MY SPARSE Ethiopian hotel room later that night. "Merry Christmas, Dad."

"Aah, Aaron . . . Merry Christmas," he said. "What's it like in Addis?"

"About 90 degrees—I'm wearing shorts and a sunburn."

"Red Rudolph nose?"

I laughed. "Actually, yes. It went great with Dubella's Santa-suit."

"Dubella?"

"He's an older boy at the orphanage. He reminds me a bit of Jordan . . . but Ethiopian."

"Oh dear."

"How is Jordan?"

"He's here. Looks good, but he hasn't changed much inside since you last saw him. Christmas Eve dinner was full of all the get rich schemes and angles he's working on."

"And chili?"

"Yes, lots of chili."

"Of course. So what tricks is Jordan up to these days?"

"He showed us pictures of several Caribbean vacations with his girlfriend."

"The stripper from his work?"

"No, a new one. He was also proud of his other toys—a convertible, a laptop, a new iPhone."

"How's he paying for all this? He hasn't had a job in nine months."

"I don't want to know," Dad said. "I just want to hear about your Christmas with the kiddos."

"It's amazing here. The trip of a lifetime," I said. "Makes me wish I was home."

"Wish you were, too."

Eleven Ethiopian tribesmen looked on as I feigned a gulp of honey wine from my cup made from a shoot of bamboo. I was in a tiny tin hut sitting on a tree-branch bench between my friends Pope (an agnostic) and Sabrina (not a teenage witch) who were convoying with me up and down the cratered roads of southern Ethiopia. Pope's and my noses were burned and redder than the rest of our white skin. Sabrina, who grew up in Zimbabwe, had a complexion of gold, like a lioness.

The orphanage in Addis Ababa was gorgeous and the kids were delightful to play with, but I wanted to branch out from the orphanage's shelter and experience the real, uncensored Ethiopia. So I met up with Pope and Sabrina, whom I'd convinced to get on a plane at London Heathrow and travel the bush with me for a week.

We went searching for gong-size sunsets and six-meter-long crocodiles and found a surplus of both. The Ethiopian sun was so large it almost set in the east as well as the west. As for the crocs, their eyeballs were as big as tennis balls that we could see bobbing above the water a hundred meters away. Our rusty boat, which was smaller than the mere tail of the Jurassic beast, floated closer and closer till we were three meters away from the monster. Then we crouched with our cameras pointed at the crocodile and snapped away. Making eye contact, the croc's tennis-ball eyes dared us to move closer, and when we didn't, his face scales ground to a grin because after surviving on Earth for the last 65 million years, he was confident his species would outlive ours.

"You like drinking tech?" one of the eleven tribesmen who had invited us to their hut asked. A striped feather, perfect like a novelty quill pen manufactured in a Chinese factory, rose from the back of his head. His name was Bekele. We all shook our bamboo cups and nodded politely. Pope was the only one actually drinking the honey wine, though. He was either braver or stupider than Sabrina and I. We'd been handed the bamboo shoots and led to the hut thirty minutes ago. It was the Festival of a Thousand Stars in Arba Minch, the annual gathering of fifty Ethiopian tribes who came together to share their dance, dress, music, tech honey wine, and raw goat meat with each other in peace. The *tukul* village of wooden huts where we were staying was hosting the closing ceremony, and thousands of tribal people whom you only see in documentaries on the National Geographic Channel mingled around the campground.

When the thousands of tribal people first arrived, we gawked at the finger-painted torsos, geometric hair shavings, three-dimensional arm tattoos in spiral shapes, and mouths with lip-plates in and lip-plates out. I never knew the plates were optional. I figured they were more permanent like pin-knees instead of being removable like shoulder pads. There is a shivering beauty though about the dangling rubber band quality of the mouths that hung from these women's chins. As I fondled my own lower lip, a man with six ivory earrings summoned us, and we followed the reflective white circles drawn on his shoulder blade to the tin hut.

"More *tech* to drink OK?" Bekele asked. He had already removed the blue lid to the 55-gallon drum of homemade liquor.

"Iyyy, no no," Sabrina said, covering her cup with her palm. "No, it is very sweet and good but we have enough." She tipped back her cup so the tangy cool liquid touched her upper lip but did not allow it to pass through.

"Maybe I will," said Pope with a swig.

"Iyyyyy, Pope. You sure you want to do that?"

"Yeah, this stuff tastes great."

"Where you from?" a man sitting on a tree branch bench across from us asked.

"U.S.A."

"George Double-Vu Boosh," a tribesman with a turquoise headband groaned into his bamboo cup. His plaid shirt was baggy and unbuttoned to the bottom of his ribs. His torso could have been on the cover of *Men's Health*.

"No!" Bekele interjected. "No more Boosh. Baraaack Obaaama!"

All eleven tribesmen held up their cups. "Baraaack Obaaaaamaa!"

Bekele, a twenty-year-old who left his village to study medicine so he could return in the future and care for the people in his community who had no doctor, reached in his pants for his Velcro wallet. He flipped it open to the clear flap designed to hold a driver's license or photo of a girlfriend and sat beside us on the bench. "You know this man?"

The future president grinned at me through the plastic film. A colorless mole lingered around his left nostril.

"He is my friend," Bekele says.

"Oh yeah? Mine too," I said.

Our bamboo cups now empty (Pope's from consumption and Sabrina's and mine from enough *oops-did-I-just-miss-my-mouth?* spills between our legs), the three of us left the hut while the eleven tribesmen trailed behind us. Outside, on a clifftop that overlooked the millions of jungle trees that lived in the Nechisar National Park, the tribes had begun to dance. A bonfire roasting hens sparked neon orange in the night. Above the embers, the constellation Orion lay on his side, sleeping on the equator through the chanting, stomping, jumping, warbling, hip-thrusting, lip-flopping, shoulder-wagging dance bursting below. There were no speakers, no synthesizer bass track. The only melody was the warble of fifty tribal tongues, and the rhythm was the pounded earth, beating under the force of our prides. Sabrina, Pope, and I danced in the middle of it all and soon everyone forgot to remember who was Hamer, Banna, Konso, or Nebraskan. Together, we were dancers, unaware of history or politics, oblivious to the malarial mosquitoes sipping from our veins, undaunted by where we would be tomorrow, because for the time being, we strangers from opposite worlds could unite and share our common humanity.

The next morning, standing under the shade of an acacia tree on the side of a savannah road, Sabrina twirled a turquoise tiara around her thumb. We were waiting for Pope to finish fertilizing the Ethiopian soil with the side effects of drinking too much contaminated honey wine. Thankfully, we couldn't see him, but the half-dozen bush tribesmen gathered around the termite mound he had hoped to hide behind were in our plain view. They seemed to be critiquing his squatting position.

"I forgot you got engaged last night, Sabrina," I said.

She placed the turquoise beads, given to her by a tribesman the way a big-city banker gives his fiancée a Tiffany ring, on top of her grainy teff-colored hair. "It's cool, hey?" she said and grinned at the memory of being crowned queen of the National Geographic Prom.

"Bekele gave me a chunk of raw goat hamstring," I said.

"That's sweet. I'd rather have my tiara."

We heard Pope say, "See you guys later," as he came around the termite mound and buckled his belt. His slow footsteps kicked up a cloud of dry dirt. His onlookers dispersed.

"Last night was killer . . . best night of my life maybe. But no more drinking *tech* . . . ever," he said when he joined us under the shady acacia.

THIRTEEN MINUTES INTO HIS PRESIDENCY on Inauguration Day, Barack Obama said, "We are shaped by every language and culture, drawn from every end of this Earth; and because we have tasted the bitter swill of civil war and segregation, and emerged from that dark chapter stronger and more united, we cannot help but believe that the old hatreds shall someday pass; that the lines of tribe shall soon dissolve; that as the world grows smaller, our common humanity shall reveal itself."

Four million double-layered gloved hands boomed in the freezing blue air. A rib-to-rib human quilt swathed the National Mall. I was too cold to feel cold anymore but, looking at the panorama of hope waving from the Capitol steps to Abraham Lincoln's memorial, I got fresh chills. I tightened the scarf around my neck. It was white with a blue and black pattern at both ends. My friend Yohannes had given it to me on my final day in Ethiopia.

Yohannes told me he was watching the speech, too, 7,000 miles away in the hotel lobby where we had first bonded to Beyoncé's "Single Ladies." He worked the night shift at the hotel where I was staying beside the orphanage. On average he worked ninety hours a week to make enough money to pay for college and support his family. I was the only guest staying in the hotel, so he was able to spend every evening with me talking about our homelands and playing mankala with peanuts because we didn't have a bag of marbles to use. On Christmas night, Yohannes beat me at mankala four games in a row.

"You is letting me win," he said.

"No, I wouldn't do that. Maybe you're eating the peanuts and cheating."

"I would not be doing that either."

"I think I'm just bad at mankala."

"Will you come to my house tomorrow for lunch? I can take you there after I finish the shift. You can meet my father."

"Where do you live?"

"In mountains on the edge of Addis. It is very nice there."

"Are you sure?"

"Sure? What is sure?"

"Uhm, it is really OK that I come to your house?"

"Oh yes, oh yes. That is being sure."

"OK, yeah. I'd love to. That's so nice, Yohannes."

While 2 million people walked the stony streets to work the next morning, Yohannes and I walked to his home. He was twenty-one and shorter, like his vocal cords, which made his voice chirp higher than most. His cheeks were naturally clean-shaven and he couldn't grow sideburns if he tried. The only spot on his face where he could was a thin strip of hair, a black milk moustache, on his upper lip. Combed clouds of brown curls capped the six sides of his angular face, sweet like honeycomb. His smile was frequent and white from the wooden stick he used to clean his teeth like a toothbrush. After a two-hour trek we arrived in his shanty village on the mountainous border of the city. He strode confidently, proud to be with me on his turf. I was proud to be with him.

"People are staring at us, huh," he said.

"Don't know why. Do you think we stand out?"

"You are the one looking as Harry Potter."

"I look like Harry Potter?"

"Yes. That is how you are looking."

Yohannes curved me right and down a craggy alley. At the end of the path he pushed aside a cutout aluminum door and I followed him through. A yellow dog named Jack ran through the sandy courtyard toward us. A few homes with open doors encircled the courtyard. They were made of rows of sticks stacked on top of each other with plaster smeared on the outside to glue them together. Yohannes plopped into a maroon armchair inside the main room of his house, which dually acted as living room and bedroom for the family of five. There were two of these armchairs and a three-seat sofa crammed into the multipurpose room. A crisply made double bed with a chrysanthemum-bottomed bedspread rested in the room's only empty corner. The furniture was so worn the Salvation

Army wouldn't have accepted it as a donation. *So this is how Michelle and Jordan would have lived had they not lived with me in the States.*

Yohannes looked at me apologetically, and I sat on the corner of the bed, hoping my face showed all the appreciation I felt toward him and not the guilt I felt about my whiney thoughts of how uncomfortable my bed at the hotel was when I woke up.

"You like music videos?" he asked. He loaded a pirated DVD into the player and I gaped in awe at the maneuvers of the Ethiopian dancers and recognized a couple of moves from the tribal night in the Ethiopian rainforest. The men's arms flailed as if there were no bones beneath the skin, and the women rolled their heads in circles faster than a tumble dryer.

"Can you pop your shoulder like that guy, Yohannes?"

He could.

"Try, Aa-ron."

I couldn't.

"What do your parents do?"

"My mom is died. My dad . . . here . . ." He pulled back the off-white veil sheet that separated the front from the back of the house. It was darker back there—the only light peeped in through cracks in the wooden door. A nest of cooking ashes clustered in the middle of the floor. Against one wall was a neat stack of the family's belongings. Along the other was a weaving loom.

"Oh wow, your dad weaves."

"Yes, weaver. Gabis . . . shawls."

The back door opened and shone more light on the contents piled beside the wall. All the family's clothes and foods and coffee-making supplies huddled together. Yohannes's two younger sisters entered the house wearing "NC State" and "Soul Falcons" sweatshirts. His older brother had his own place, he told me. The girls started preparing lunch on the floor.

"Yohannes, can I use your um, bathroom?"

Blank stare.

"Washroom? Loo?"

Eyebrows up.

Then finally the word I didn't want to use because I assumed there wasn't one. "Toilet?"

"Ah, ishee." He led me out back and pointed to a shed.

The latch to the tin latrine was a wooden block. A Coca-Cola bottle cap was pinned to it for decoration. I spun the latch locked. Standing on the floor of 2 × 4's with a hole cut out in the middle, I contemplated just how I was going to do this without making a mess of things, and my mind jumped back to Jordan eighteen years ago, surrounded by porcelain, sitting in a urinal, contemplating the same thing. *This is what every minute of his life felt like—vulnerable, helpless, unsure, naked.* But it was probably only a nick of what his life felt like. He was a child and I was a privileged adult white male with a return plane ticket already printed in my bag beside all the creature comforts I had packed for my short stay.

I unlatched the door to Yohannes's latrine. Finished. I had probably done it all wrong.

"It's not very nice, is it?" Yohannes said when I returned.

"It's like that in most of Nebraska, too," I lied. "Can I see the sketches you were telling me about?"

He slid his green folder that contained his portfolio out from under the bed. The first piece, drawn when he was eleven, was of Mickey and Minnie holding helium balloons that spelled "Yohannes" in Amharic text. Then a series of pencil-shaded life-size hands holding an eraser, a paintbrush, a cigarette. Next a nude man with a Michelangelo-inspired back—muscle on top of twisting muscle. "Michelangelo is so amazing artist," Yohannes says. Farrah Fawcett, shoes, a wine bottle.

"These are beautiful."

He flipped over the last sheet in the folder. It was the penciled profile of a horse, silver and perfect. Its one visible eye was tired but intent.

"Yohannes, I love this."

"You have it. Have it with you."

I argued until he said, "It is an honor if you have it with you."

"Ahmasaygunalo. Thank you. Really. Will you show me your school sketches, too?"

When he was not working the night shift or showing a Harry Potter look-alike around Addis, Yohannes studied architecture at Addis Ababa University. He handed me his graph pad and there, sitting in a two-room shanty that once slept six, I examined the blueprints of three-story, four-bath houses wrapped in windows.

"Are there houses like these in Ethiopia?"

"Some. I will be having one someday."

Jack the dog barked.

"Oh! Father is coming home," Yohannes said, and I stood one moment later as he entered. We shook right hands, holding our own wrists with our left out of respect. Then he put his arm around his son, whose arching black milk moustache flattened out as he smiled.

The sisters brought in a mound of red ground *firfir* on an *injera* sticky bread platter and we three men huddled around. While we pinched the *firfir* with the spongy bread, the girls began the coffee ceremony on the floor. They'd already roasted the coffee beans on the fire and crushed them in the back room. Now, as the grounds brewed in a kettle, the older sister ignited the urn of incense with a hot coal. Dense sugary smoke overwhelmed the room, and I had to pause to focus on breathing.

Yohannes's dad told him something in Amharic and gestured at me.

"Eat, Aaa-ron. Eat more," Yohannes translated. Even in Ethiopia.

We finished lunch and drank Ethiopian black coffee from a mix 'n' match tea set. Yohannes and his father drank the fire-hot steroid-strong cups like shots of whiskey. I had to sip my first cup to practice. I shot the next two.

"You are getting better."

I was. Euphorically better. Maybe it was the caffeine in my veins or the incense fumes in my lungs, but I couldn't remember being better, welcomer, happier.

"I am very lucky to be with you today," I said. "It's an honor."

Yohannes fluttered behind the veil and returned with a white *gabi.* A blue and black pattern ornamented both ends. He draped it around my neck.

Back on America's National Mall, I inhaled the freezing blue sky, and it smelled of the sugary incense sprinkled on the scarf wrapped tightly beneath my nose. The scent had faded some but it was there; an everlasting ode to the happy day a young man in Ethiopia shared with a young man from America.

"And to those nations like ours that enjoy relative plenty, we say we can no longer afford indifference to the suffering outside our borders; nor can we consume the world's resources without regard to effect. For the world has changed, and we must change with it."

He's right, Obama. The world is different. People on our planet are more connected in more ordinary ways every day than ever before. Or at least ever since our original ancestors started migrating out of Ethiopia millions of years ago.

I encountered many examples of this shift on my journey. There were three nationalities working together to save a boy's life in a Chinese restaurant on Christmas Eve in Addis Ababa. A Christian-raised white boy rowed a boat along India's Ganga River as Hindus, Buddhists, and Muslims bathed in the rancid holy water they believe gives life to the entire universe, and Koreans and non-Koreans lived together on a peninsula that had boxed out the rest of the planet for centuries. More than ever, we belong to each other.

International adoption is one more example of this belonging, but I needed to experience the others to see it that way. In 2008, 17,438 international orphans were united with their families in the United States. They are united by the feeling that in 1999 kept me awake all night watching *Clueless* with Michelle, doing what I could to help my sister from the other side of the world survive one more time. A sense of connection that in 1988 inspired Mom and Dad to set pen to paper and key to typewriter ribbon and start a global family. My siblings and I were not normal—maybe we were just a little ahead of the times, like an early mutation in the chain of the world's evolution.

WHILE LISTENING TO THE BEATLES on the radio and picturing himself in a boat on a river with tangerine trees and marmalade skies in 1974, archaeologist Donald Johanson discovered the fossils of a girl with bipedal legs in northern Ethiopia. He named her Lucy, after the song. She was the first known *Australopithecus afarensis* (a short, hairy, upright-walking human-monkey) and is believed to be the evolutionary ancestor of *Homo sapiens.* Basically, she is your and my great-grandmother times almost infinity.

In modern-day Ethiopia, Lucy's homeland descendants are the three-year-olds running in packs through the street. Dark patches ring the skin on their shoulders where the seams of their shirts have ripped open.

They are the five-year-olds playing foosball outside of shops who shouted, "Gimme dollar. Gimme pen. Gimme pie!" as I passed and gave them a thumbs-up before they upped one back.

They are also the nine-year-old blue minibus operators who tried to have entire conversations with me using strictly the word *ishee.*

"Ishee."

"Ishee?"

"Eh, ishee."

"Ishee ishee."

"Ishee . . ."

Just like the children of one-child China before it, caste-system India before it, homogeneous Korea before it, Manhattan's Five Points slum before it, and the dockyards of Georgian London before it, the millions of orphans in overpopulated, poorer-than-poor, AIDS- and malaria-stricken Ethiopia are—for lack of a more appropriate word—fucked.

Domestic adoption isn't a feasible solution because life is struggle enough for most Ethiopian families without having another stomach to fill and brain to nourish. Stigma surrounds the abandoned children of unwed mothers. The government spends $400 million a year on its military and $140 million on health. But like China, India, Korea, Manhattan, and London's East End, there is hope for Ethiopia.

As Charles Darwin's *Origin of Species* revealed 150 years ago, all it takes is a variation, an adaptation to environmental factors that might increase an individual's chances of survival. Darwin's idea of a variation referred to a freak mutation in a species' DNA, but it speaks just as much for a bend in a species' conscience.

There are moments in history when mankind has the chance to choose mutation, invert evolution, reverse nature, and make an apple fall up from the tree. Just like foundling hospitals for abandoned babies and trains for orphaned children in earlier centuries, international adoption offers humanity one such chance to trump nature and choose our history. Now Ethiopia has that chance as it opens its borders to global adoption.

Even though international adoption once saved his life, what Jordan chose to do with his chance is less inspiring. It is mysterious, though. Mom and Dad asked themselves if it was their parenting that caused Jordan's failing. Or perhaps his slip stemmed from some psychological trauma embedded in his brain from living on the streets in India when he was three. Or maybe he was just an upward-falling *bad* apple all along. But I don't think so.

I believe Jordan is the way he is for the same reason he is still walking about on the earth and not buried dead below. He is a naturally selected survivor. Before his fifth birthday he managed to live when both of his birth parents were gone. He conquered an infection that was powerful enough to kill him. He acclimated to a foreign world where the only thing that was familiar to him was Michelle. And then she went away, too, after a lifetime of protecting him.

Jordan never entirely let go of his survival instincts when he settled into life in Nebraska—they were simply applied to his new endeavors. He was always looking for fast ways to get himself ahead.

"Hold down these buttons all at once and then press your floor number," he told Dad in the elevator at Dad's office.

"Why, Jordan?"

"It will take you there express now and won't stop on any of the other floors."

"What if somebody needed to get on the elevator on the fifth floor?"

"So?"

"So that's not right."

"But we need to get to the seventh." Jordan pressed the button combination and we whizzed to Dad's floor.

Then when I turned sixteen and passed my driving exam, I began helping Mom and Dad with taxi duty when they were at work. On Tuesdays and Thursdays after picking Meredith up from elementary school at 3:45, I would speed to get Jordan to basketball practice by four o'clock. He had to do a lap for every minute he was late, so Jordan took the drive very seriously.

"You should have accelerated at that yellow light, Aaron."

"You don't have to pay the fines if I get a ticket, Jordan."

"OK, then flash your brights."

"How will blinking my headlights get you to basketball on time?"

"Flash 'em. You'll trick the stoplight into thinking you're an ambulance and it will turn green."

"I'm not an ambulance, though."

"Just try it."

I flashed the brights on my little red Neon. The light turned green.

"Told you."

Until Michelle was moved to Uta Halee, Jordan's survival schemes were innocent enough. Then they started to become criminal. The police rang the doorbell to bring Jordan home after he was caught breaking into cars. Later, Dad found drug paraphernalia in Jordan's room. Even when Jordan showed up late and stoned to our Grandma Eske's funeral, Mom and Dad still didn't have it in them to pull him out of the downward spiral. He was testing them to see if his way of life in our home was in jeopardy after Michelle had been, as he saw it, removed from our family. Mom and Dad failed his test. All their energy was devoted to saving Michelle from her demons, and they no longer had the will to save Jordan from his. For the second time in Jordan and Michelle's lives, their parents were forced to choose one child to sacrifice so the other could be rescued. This time, Michelle won the coin toss.

The day after Jordan graduated from high school, Dad drove him to the army recruitment office to enlist. Mom and Dad's thinking at the time was that Jordan needed discipline that they could no longer emotionally provide him. Then maybe he could get his life back on track. The army denied Jordan admission. He failed the drug test. Every two weeks after the first attempt, Dad drove Jordan back to the recruitment center and they would try again. And every time Jordan's pee would show traces of some new drug use, no matter how many nutritional supplements he had taken to trick the test. After three months, the test finally came back clean, and the next day Jordan boarded a once-yellow school bus that had been painted camouflage green and was taken away to basic training boot camp.

Everyone in the family except me attended Jordan's cadet graduation six months later. I had moved out east to Washington, D.C., for an internship and couldn't pay for the airplane ticket to the ceremony. Well, to be honest, I could have afforded it if I had given up happy hours for the month, but by then I had done more than move out of Nebraska. I had also moved on and decided that spending nights at bars with my coworkers would bring me more joy than seeing Jordan walk across a stage in a uniform.

Perhaps it was the pageantry, the row of flags, or the hundreds of look-alike buzz haircuts, but Dad felt a sense of pride looking up at Jordan in the auditorium. He knew it was a false feeling, like the tingles you get when a gold medal–winning American gymnast does a flawless floor routine to the song "I'm Proud to Be an American," but he clung to it nonetheless. Jordan's life was going up again. After the graduation ceremony, my family went to the Olive Garden for dinner. Jordan, dressed from hat to boot in camouflage green military gear, held the front door for the other guests as they entered. He had chosen the restaurant. Made the reservation in advance even. He sat tall in his seat and politely asked for Meredith to pass the salad bowl. She did and smiled across the table at him, happy to have a brother back.

"Thank you, Jordan," Mom said hugging him goodbye.

"For what?"

"For today. For doing what it took to get to today."

A month later, Jordan called home from his base in Fort Benning, Georgia, and told Dad he wanted to take night classes at Troy State University.

"That sounds great, Jordan."

"I need some money for a laptop to do homework and a car to drive to class, though."

"That's OK. I think we can do that. How much do you need?"

Three months after Jordan cashed the check, he called home again. This time from prison.

"Dad?"

"What happened, Jordan?"

"Uhm . . . see . . . I'm in jail."

"Why? What did you do?"

"Nothing, it's not my . . ."

"People aren't arrested for no reason, Jordan."

"It's a D.U.I."

The next day an army sergeant called Dad with an update. They had gone into Jordan's room to inspect for other incriminating evidence.

"What did you find?" Dad asked.

"More drugs," the Sergeant said. "We think he might be selling."

"I thought he was going in a good direction. I actually believed him. But it was just another one of his shams, wasn't it?"

"You know what would'a caused him to start this, sir?"

Then Dad remembered Jordan's schemes and realized what was happening. "Are any units shipping off to Iraq soon?"

"We're always deploying, sir."

"There's your reason. He's just surviving."
"Excuse me? I don't follow."
"He can't die in Iraq if he's locked up in jail."

~

THREE AND A HALF MILLION YEARS after her death, the fossils of Lucy the *Australopithecus afarensis* still resided in Ethiopia—in the Addis Ababa National History Museum. The museum kept the old girl encased in glass in the basement. The lights down there were dim, and the walls were reinforced with thin sheets of plywood that didn't block the sounds of construction on the street outside. I went to pay my respects to my family's oldest ancestor and wondered if she hummed songs or kissed her boyfriend(s).

Gazing down at the brown bones, I saw another woman's reflection in the glass. A yellow bandana restrained her blond hair from her eyes. An Ethiopian baby boy was strapped to her chest and she cooed to him, the best Christmas present she could ask for, her adopted son, her upward-falling apple, the newest member of her 3.5-million-ring-old family tree. "Je t'aime," she whispered and kissed the top of his fuzzy head.

Chapter Eleven

HOMECOMINGS

When a Californian does something notable—stars in a movie, wins a Nobel Prize, hits a home run—other Californians don't know. Nebraskans don't forget. We cling to the rare remarkable achievements of our natives. When you get a drink at what used to be George's Bar before George died a few years back in Wahoo, Nebraska, a woman named Joyce might tell you how the townspeople convinced late-night talk show host David Letterman to name Wahoo his official "Home Office," a half-hour's drive from Omaha. While ever-shifting her above-average weight on an average barstool, she'll tell you how they got the Nebraska Unicameral to make Dave an admiral in the Great Navy of the State of Nebraska, and sent him some flowers, letters, cow pies, a nifty wall clock. Joyce laughs, low like a smoker, contagious like the flu.

With her hand on your shoulder and her eyes on her husband, who has a dog's nickname and a drinking problem older than his wife, she'll call out to him at the far side of the bar. "Hey Buster!

C'm'ere! I want you to meet somebody." Then when he doesn't look up from his glass, she'll squeeze your shoulder, say "Maybe next time, blue eyes," and before you have a chance to ask the question that wasn't on your mind, she'll tell you about Warren Buffett's billions, Charley Starkweather's eleven, Tommy Frazier's touchdowns, Dick Cheney's childhood, Malcolm X's disobedience, Johnny Carson's jokes. Then she'll astound you and describe Willa Cather's prose. But you shouldn't be astonished. Every Nebraskan who graduated eighth grade knows her prose.

Booksellers across the state display Willa's masterpiece *My Ántonia* in their shop windows almost a century after it was first published. The novel is the prairie story of a narrator named Jim whose life intersects with that of an orphan girl named Ántonia when they immigrate to Nebraska as children. The two are close in age and become best friends. When he grows up, Jim goes away to Harvard and deserts Ántonia but not his memory of her.

Before moving to London, I bought a used copy of *My Ántonia* and read it on the airplane over the Atlantic Ocean. When I turned to the book's last page, the text was highlighted in yellow by its past owner. I knew that part. It was the passage where Jim returns to Nebraska twenty years after he departed. A moved-on man, he says:

> This was the road over which Ántonia and I came on that night when we got off the train at Black Hawk and were bedded down in the straw, wondering children, being taken we knew not whither. I had only to close my eyes to hear the rumbling of the wagons in the dark, and to be again overcome by that obliterating strangeness. The feelings of that night were so near that I could reach out and touch them with my hand. I had the sense of coming home to myself, and of having found out what a little circle man's experience is. For Ántonia and for me, this had been the road of Destiny; had taken us to those early accidents of fortune which predetermined for us

> all that we can ever be. Now I understood that the same road was to bring us together again. Whatever we had missed, we possessed together the precious, the incommunicable past.[1]

HONG KONG INTERNATIONAL AIRPORT was busy. Busier than the usual 1 million passengers it ushers in and out of its grand terminals each day. The world was coming to China for the 2008 Summer Olympic Games. I was leaving; flying home after a year abroad. I had been in Hong Kong for Beijing's opening-ceremony-slash-holy-shit spectacular the night before. Downtown, the city's skyscrapers were outfitted with jumbo screens and loudspeakers and at 8:00 PM on August 8, 2008, the explosion of 2,008 fou drums hushed the thousands of pedestrians walking about the clean streets at dusk. We all halted, enchanted, to stare at the nearest jumbo screen. We sat on the sidewalk, sat in the street, it didn't matter. The drums paralyzed the whole city and, from reports, they paralyzed the whole world. Depending on where you read your news, between 1 billion and 4 billion people on Earth heard those 2,008 drums.

The loudspeaker at the airport called my flight's final boarding. "All remaining passengers for American Airlines Flight 6120 to Los Angeles, we request that you please board at this time." I wasn't postponing getting on the 747 because I felt reluctant to leave Asia . . . well maybe a little reluctant but that wasn't it. And it wasn't that I hated sitting on airplanes so much that I waited at the gate until the last minute the way some people do. After traveling from London to Delhi to Agra to Varanasi to Pune to Mumbai to Seoul to the DMZ to Kyoto to Tokyo to Hong Kong, the coach section was my living room. It was the place I felt most at home. Except for now in the Hong Kong airport terminal where an American couple wearing XXL Chicago Cubs T-shirts fumbled with their first daughter, a nine-month-old Chinese girl in yellow socks.

I haven't mentioned it yet because my nuclear family is big enough, but my cousins were also internationally adopted from China and lived in Chicago. Because of the age difference between me and them, I don't know much about the girls other than that Shannon, who's nine, loves horses and her little sister, Kiley, doesn't like sleeping alone. Their parents, my aunt and uncle, were physically quite different from the Cubs couple in the terminal. But both sets of parents looked at their daughters the same way. I peeked at the XXL set in between page turns of the book I was reading. They probably noticed me but didn't care; just like my parents didn't care about the hundreds of eyes staring at us in Minneapolis when Michelle and Jordan exited their aircraft in 1991 and piled into Dad's silver Buick.

THE STREETLIGHTS WERE ON WHEN I landed in Los Angeles. Hundreds of thousands of them. Toenail picked me up in a maroon four-door Honda. It was a gross nickname but so were his toenails after twenty-six years of not wearing shoes. He was a flip-flop man—one of the main reasons he moved to California from Nebraska after college—and it showed in the dirt beneath his cuticles.

"You must be exhausted," Toenail said.

"I'm fine."

"But that flight's 14 hours."

"Fifteen."

"You don't want to sleep?"

"Let's go to West Hollywood."

"You want to go out? Really, after all that?"

"Toenail, I don't know what time or day it is."

"It's Friday at midnight."

I laughed.

"What?"

"Yesterday when I got on the plane it was Friday at midnight."

"You need to sleep."

"I need to America. To remember what it's like."

We drove down Sunset Boulevard, passing the Cinerama Dome where I worked for a summer a few years earlier. I scooped popcorn for movie premieres. Popcorn for Heather Locklear, Frodo Baggins, Paris Hilton, Tom Cruise, Tom Cruise's alleged gay porn star lover. The classic theater was shaped like a colossal igloo and was a relic of a time gone by when Americans threatened with nuclear obliteration would go to a movie and find solace in the dark drinking a 25-cent Pepsi. I could now relate. I did the same thing after a week in Delhi, except the havoc I was hiding from was India, and the cinema was a concrete block with ceiling fans the size of wind turbines.

In Delhi, I paid 75 cents to see the nine o'clock *Kismat Konnection,* a Bollywood chick flick about luck, with an auditorium of Indian men who loved it. Before the show I mingled in the dirt parking lot with some of the men who had swaggered over to me to find out why a white guy was in line to see a Hindi movie. The men, my age, told me about their days peddling bicycle rickshaws and their nights sleeping on them—feet roosting on the handlebar.

So while I chewed my popcorn in the light of a movie projector reflecting off a solid white wall, the breeze of the jumbo fans blowing lukewarm air my way, I understood why they did it. Why whenever a fast happy song came on in *Kismat,* every man around me shot out of his seat to dance. They hula-hooped their hips and waved their arms. They weren't dancing together; they danced for themselves. In the dark theater, they could forget what life was like in the Delhian dirt and pretend for 153 minutes that they were lucky, too.

The rainbow flags in gay West Hollywood waved. Toenail parked the Honda. We went into a club. I reminded myself not to bow to the bouncer. The place was full of white people and only a couple of Asians. 1920s pornography, in which the women wore negligees, was projected on the wall. I ordered a vodka-cranberry. Nine dollars. One more for tip. Enough to feed a family in Pune for a week. I sipped. We danced. Toenail introduced me to his friend.

"Wow, so you like woke up in China today."

"Uh huh."

"How was your trip?"

What do I say? Where do I start? With the smell of a monsoon or the feel of the Taj Mahal? Maybe I could describe schools in slums, bath time at an orphanage, two graves on a Korean hillside. A week ago I told a Japanese man all these things at an underground gay bar in Tokyo called Arty Farty. He didn't speak English and my Japanese was limited to *konichiwa*, but his cell phone had a built-in translator that we passed back and forth for hours swapping stories. I had nothing to swap on this Californian dance floor with a stranger who wouldn't understand. He was wearing a small gray shirt that looked like mine but really was nothing like mine because mine had the muck of the world crusted into the collar, and he bought his yesterday at Abercrombie & Fitch.

"Asia was good. Fun."

"That's cool."

"Yeah."

"How long are you here?"

"L.A. for two more days and then I'm driving to Seattle."

"Man, you don't sit still. Aren't you tired?"

I was exhausted. So far I had torn off four pages of my five-page-single-spaced–10-point-font travel itinerary. Each sheet of paper was another 3,000 miles closer to home. I had never wanted to be back in Nebraska with my family this much before.

"Nope. I feel fine."

"Have a safe drive north. It's beautiful, man. I mean really fucking beautiful."

He was right about the drive. I had never experienced it before, but having the Pacific Ocean to your left and mountains to your right and redwoods to your up-and-up *was* really fucking beautiful. The plains where I grew up have no oceans or mountains or 350-foot trees. So to see all three in between two pit stops was astonishingly alien. After traveling so long, a lot was alien to me now on Route 101. Signs in English. Drivers who used turn signals. A song on the radio by some girl about kissing a girl and liking it. Fast-food drive-thrus.

IN 1991, MY NEW FAMILY STOPPED at McDonald's on the highway home from Minneapolis. Neither Jordan nor Michelle had eaten a Happy Meal before. Dad ordered three—one for each of us kids—and we sat in a row sharing one side of a booth. We leaned forward to reach the laminate table.

"One Happy Meal for Michelle. Happy Meal for Ganga."

"Oppy Meel?" Michelle repeated after Dad. "Oppy! Oppy!"

Jordan ate his french fries with his wrists. The infected scabies on the palms of his hands and fingers were green and pussy like exploded peas and sizzled when they touched salt. For real sizzled like bacon on a skillet or slugs in a bucket of sodium. The stinging didn't slow him down, though. He pinched four fries at a time between his wrists and dipped them in a pool of ketchup before aiming them at his mouth. When the box of fries was empty, Jordan shook his carton of chicken nuggets and put his nose up to the lid. I unlatched the paper clasp and poured the nuggets onto his tray. He put his wrists back together and his cheeks puffed from the amount of processed chicken he'd wedged inside.

"Whoa there, Jordan," Dad said sweetly. "No rush. One at a time or you'll choke."

"Like this, Jordan," I demonstrated with one of mine.

Jordan jabbered to Michelle in Marathi. No one knows what he said, but if I had to guess, it was probably something like, "What am I eating? Who are these pale people? Where the hell are we?"

Jordan started eating from Michelle's Happy Meal box but she didn't mind. She was preoccupied tearing into the plastic wrap so she could play with her Alvin and the Chipmunks toy.

"That's Theodore," I told her.

"Oppy meel!"

"Yeah, Happy Meal. She's learning, Mom."

"She will. It will take some time but she and Jordan will be used to everything soon."

MICHELLE LIVED IN THE Uta Halee Girls Village for nearly two years. Then she was released. When she came home to our parents' house, she no longer wanted to paint her bedroom black. She didn't want to do anything, actually. Not even an *I Love Lucy* marathon could cheer her up. Slowly, the girl I'd known growing up started to reappear—a giggle here and a dress there—but it was too late for me to see her as my sister. She and Jordan found a way to restore their bond. Same story with Meredith and Jamie. But our common ground had eroded too deeply, and we were too separated now. I had started university, my future, and I wasn't interested in the past.

During my first year at the University of Nebraska, Michelle and I used to cross paths at Mom and Dad's house some weekends. I would leave the dorms and go back a couple times a month to do my laundry and steal some food. When I was there, sitting on the couch beside the laundry room so I could be sure to hear the buzzer, I was quiet and withdrawn and when I left I felt moody. By my senior year, I only went home if it was someone's birthday, and even that took lots of reminding.

Michelle lived at the house for a while but graduated from high school a year early and moved out as soon as she could. She paid her bills by wiping butts at a nursing home. The only person in the family she spoke to was Grandmother Lenore. After half a year of the silent treatment, she reappeared at my parents' doorstep at dinnertime and said she wanted to start nursing school so she could help others in ways beyond anal hygiene. So she enrolled in Lincoln's community college and started working toward a nursing degree.

Numbers were always a foreign language to Michelle, and she struggled with her courses. She came back to Mom for help and they studied side-by-side at the dining table twenty hours a week for four years until she completed her two-year degree. Mom taught Michelle how to take a pulse, how to calculate the right medication dosages so she didn't poison a patient, and how to insert a urinary catheter into a woman's urethra and not her vagina. Luckily, Michelle's teacher overlooked that last one when she got it backwards in the final clinical exam and passed her through to the next level.

The day after Michelle graduated from nursing school in her satin blue gown, Mom called me in London. "She's my proudest accomplishment," she said. "You'd think it would be you but it's not. You turned out how you were supposed to, White Boy. But she's been defying her fate all her life."

Even though Michelle now had her degree, Mom did not retire from tutoring. She simply moved on to studying chemistry at the dining table with Michelle's boyfriend, who had gone back to school with Michelle's encouragement. While Mom was explaining to him how to balance a chemical equation like $P_4 + 5O_2 \rightarrow 2P_2O_5$, he put down his pencil.

"Come on, hang in there," Mom said.

"I don't think I can do it anymore."

"If I can get Michelle to understand pathophysiology, I can get you through Phosphorus and Oxygen."

"Deb, it's not the chemistry. It's Michelle."

"Oh."

"I can't take anymore of her mood swings. She's upset with me when I don't even do anything."

"You know why she's doing this to you, right?"

"No idea."

"She doesn't want you to leave her."

"I don't get it."

"The people who she's loved in her life have all left her . . . myself included for a little while there. She's afraid of getting hurt again. So she's taking back the control and scaring you away before you have the chance."

"Did she tell you that?"

"Nope. Didn't have to. I know her demons and I'm sorry that they've come out to stomp on your parade."

"What demons?"

"You know, her childhood."

"Oh," he picked back up his pencil.

"Oh shit. She hasn't told you yet has she."

"I guess not."

"Well I'll let her speak for herself, but you . . ."

"What can I do?"

"Don't leave her. She just needs to see you stay."

"Well, that's not a great solution, is it."

"Sorry, big guy. Life's not fair. But you have to keep on living anyway."

"You home yet? I want to cut your hair. xoxo," Meredith texted me as I drove through a giant redwood tree in northern California.

"Almost. So excited to see you! Get your trimming shears ready. I'm shaggy," I sent back.

Meredith didn't quit beauty school like she had quit university, playing the flute, dancing, all of her friendships, and everything else she had once accomplished in spite of her handicaps.

For years I attended each one of Meredith's band concerts where she sat in the front row with her flute, pressing down on the keys with her nubby fingers. She was in fifth grade the first time she performed on the flute for an audience. Mom let her wear makeup that night, which she put on her face herself. The silver eye shadow was chalky white on her brown skin and she applied so many layers of lipstick that it rubbed red all over her instrument's mouthpiece as she puckered her lips to play the Beach Boys' "Surfin' U.S.A.," the staple anthem for every beginner band. If I hadn't played the song myself on trombone when I was in fifth grade, I might not have recognized the tune. It sounded like mush. Except for Meredith on her lipstick-smeared flute who hit every high note in perfect rhythm. She was first-chair flutist in every concert after that all the way through high school. Then she earned a prestigious slot in the nation's top band for young musicians. And then she quit.

She had become a cheerleader instead, opting to be at the pinnacle of popularity. Meredith was the only girl on the squad who didn't have to go to Tan Zone to get the cancerous bronzed skin the others yearned for. She was also the only girl whose legs looked like tubes of salami that had been tied up with tight string. It didn't take long for the other teenagers to notice Meredith's birth abnormalities and make her feel inferior because of them in the locker room, on the football field sidelines, and at the homecoming dance. Her whole life she had deflected the occasional attacks and smirks aimed at the body she was born with and had grown to overcome. But she wasn't strong enough to defend her hormonal emotions against a relentless pack of sixteen-year-old girls.

I was in college and out of my family's house when Meredith began to lose her way. Then I was across the country and then across the ocean. It made me sad to see but I had no idea how to help so I didn't try. I virtually watched her wander, though, from the random sampling of posts she wrote on her Facebook wall:

Meredith is how much bad news can one person get in a day? . . . i would know

Meredith is fuck my life!!!! i mean really can things get any worse?

Meredith is reading My Sisters Keeper.

Meredith is sick and they dont know whats wrong and my tongue is swelling up . . . i don't think this could get any worse. . . .

Meredith is reading Plain Truth

Meredith went from being "single" to "in a relationship."

Meredith is wishes things weren't the way they are right noww . . .

Meredith went from being "in a relationship" to "single."

Meredith is reading The Pact.

Meredith is excited to see her big brother this weekend!!!! :)

Meredith is reading Perfect Match

Meredith is alone in this world so big

Meredith is not dropping out of college it just didn't work out for her but thanks to those great friends who r telling everyone that i dropped out! thanks!

Meredith is dusting the dirt off her pants and standing back up on her own two feet again.

It might still be a while before she can get all the dirt off, but Meredith really has been learning to put down the depressing Jodi Picoult novels and stand up for herself again. After enrolling in beauty school, she moved into her own apartment with roommates. A few weeks before she took and passed her state cosmetology examination, an Indian man came in wanting a haircut. While she trimmed his bangs, he noticed her deformed fingers working in front of his eyes.

"Oh yeah, those," she said, repositioning her cutting shears in her hand to get a better grip. "I was born that way. But when I was adopted we got my fingers snipped apart in surgery so now I can cut hair!"

"No wonder your birth mother gave you up with fingers like those," he said.

"Excuse me?"

"You brought shame to your Indian mother. That is why she had to abandon you."

"You know what? I have beautiful hands and a family who loves me," Meredith said as she chopped a thick chunk of black hair from the back of the man's head, flung off the black nylon apron that covered his torso, and showed him the door.

Her inner fire was not what it had been before, but at least the pilot light was burning again.

I STOPPED DRIVING FOR THE NIGHT in Eugene, a small city with lots of big trees. It was also home to the University of Oregon and Holt International's headquarters where Bertha Holt went to work for the second half of the twentieth century. Early the next day as the sun was shepherding away the morning fog, I checked out of the hotel but didn't immediately ride up the ramp to the Interstate. First I visited the Holt office.

The receptionist gave me a formal tour of the building. It felt more like a home than an office. We walked down the cushy carpeted staircase to the lower level. Groups of cubicles with calendars of adopted children pinned to the felt walls were nested in the center of the room. Along the real wall was a steel door, eight inches thick and ajar.

"What's that?" I asked, pointing at the door.

"Oh, it's our vault."

"Like a bank?"

"I suppose. It's where we keep the paperwork of every child who has ever been adopted into the Holt family."

"All 50,000?"

"Go on in. You'll see."

Yes. All 50,000. Rows of shelves that touched the ceiling were stuffed with multicolored folders—one for each family.

"The vault has a combination and we lock it each night before we go home. It is fireproof as well so nothing bad can happen to these memories."

Looking at all the folders together was like beholding the orderly mass of white headstones in Arlington Cemetery and realizing the enormity of war in a way you can't achieve by watching a show on the History Channel.

"Can I see my family's file?"

"That's what it's here for. Your last name is Eske, correct?"

"Yes. E-S-K-E."

"You'll be over here, then." I followed her far down the third row until she stopped and slid out a green folder. "I'll give you a few minutes with this if you'd like."

Holding it in my hands like a book, I opened the file and flipped through its photocopied pages. Mom and Dad's adoption applications in cursive and typewriter. Pictures of Meredith's twisted ankles taken by her nurse in India. Police referral papers with the names Ganga and Bhola written up top in English and Hindi. A letter addressed to Michelle and Jordan in the orphanage and signed by me. Photographs of Meredith and me sitting in the sprinklers, the three Indians posing in traditional garb on the staircase in the pink house, Jordan showing off his heart catheter, and Michelle and me standing in front of a fountain at Disney World. They were all images Mom and Dad must have mailed to Holt over the years to prove they hadn't lost any of their children or shipped them back. The final photocopies in the folder were the forms filled out by Jamie's foster mother for every month Jamie lived with her in Korea. I recognized the Hangul snowmen calligraphy and missed it after just a few days of being away.

I missed all of it; all of them. Had I had that green folder before my journey, I would have read through it and kept it somewhere safe. But I wouldn't have felt connected to its contents the way I did after I had seen where they came from. The same was true of the whole vault. Somewhere in there was a folder for a family like mine in 1956. My guess is, there will also be a folder for a family like mine in 2056 that will adopt a child from a country that due to poverty or war is unable to support all its children on its own.

Humanity has come a long way. For starters, we take care of orphans. We try to find them families that live across town or across three oceans because our love has grown bigger than our backyards. And once children are in those families, we talk about how they were adopted, and we don't pretend they weren't. These are all fairly new and radical advancements.

Yet international adoption is not perfect and it might never be. The only ideal scenario is for a child to never become an orphan. Until we can figure out how to universally make that dream real, international adoption is a beautiful solution. However, just because it is loving at its core does not mean we can let down our guard. International adoption's motives and economics are sometimes wrinkled.

And its effects on orphaned children and the families that adopt them can be flammable.

My family was not alone in our distress. The sad and unseen truth is that a child with a tortured past is not likely to have a carefree future no matter where you move him or how many toys she opens on her birthday. International adoption is not a delete key. You cannot undo a child's trauma, only prepare for it to resurface. There are millions of older orphans who know torture so brutal that only now can I begin to reluctantly imagine their endurance.

Even children who are internationally adopted as infants are not spared from personal crises because we live in a society that preys on identities that are different. These children will face adversity. But remember, it's not the first time they've had to overcome a challenge to survive.

"You ready to move on?" the Holt receptionist asked as I held close the paperwork that recorded my family's creation.

"Yeah," I said and gently set the file back on the shelf beside the others.

Seoul's Gyeongbokgung Palace was built during the Joseon Dynasty in 1394, but it still shines like a box of wax crayons even on a cloudy day. Intricate lotus flowers in rose, lilac, mint, and lemon pigment trim the exterior of the ten buildings. The roofs swoop like petals. The palace is flawless. At least what's left of it. Before the Japanese demolished 97 percent of the structure in 1911, there were 330 such buildings. Gravel courtyards now grace the 4,414,000 square feet of land where they once stood. As Jamie shuffled through the courtyards and back 600 years in time, she retrieved her Clinique compact to inspect her new teenage complexion.

Jamie and my parents kicked off their Reeboks and walked around the royal throne of Korea in their socks. Dad filmed every step. When they completed the circle, they jammed their feet back in their shoes. They'd begun the day untying the laces but stopped after the seventh time.

"Now the Folk Museum?"

"Do we hafta?"

"Yes. They're your folk and we should see them."

Reeboks crunched the gravel on the walk to the nearby museum of all things culturally Korean. Inside, Jamie pretended to care about the ancient pottery—about how the porcelain jars were left undecorated to showcase their purity, a purity derived from a compound of feldspathic rocks and hot, hot fire. She even faked her way through Korean hats of the ages. At the window display about first birthdays in Korea, called *tol,* she actually read the plaque explaining the *tol-bok* outfits and ritual rice cake feast—steamed rice for divinity, red bean powder rice for health, sticky rice for tenacity.

"Mom, I turned one in Korea, didn't I?"

"Yep. With your foster family."

On her first birthday, Jamie (or Yoo Jung Choi, as her foster mother knew her) wore a *jogory* silk jacket with striped sleeves the same color as the lotus flowers on the Gyeongbokgung. Her foster mother bought it for her. She also prepared mounds of rice cakes, fruit, jujubes, and noodles (long for longevity) and set them before the child she'd cared for almost from the beginning, eleven months before, back when Jamie wasn't supposed to survive to celebrate her *tol.*

"You can ask them about it tomorrow when we meet them."

That was why Mom and Dad had taken Jamie to Korea—to meet her foster family. Their search for Jamie's origins was not timed with mine but, as I said, Dad taped almost every minute of their week in Korea so I didn't even need to be there. He had recently bought a new camcorder to replace the one that used to get so much footage but hadn't been out much since Jamie came home from Korea the first time.

At 8:58 the next morning, Jamie peered in the glass doors of Lotte's, Korea's twelve-story version of Harrod's department store. The doors were still locked, but the clerks buzzed around inside finishing last-minute tasks.

"Isn't it 9 yet?"

"We're early."

A Korean woman waiting as well approached Jamie and spoke to her some admonishing words in Hangul.

"What are you saying?" Jamie asked. "I'm American. I mean I'm Korean . . . but I'm American."

"괜찮아." The woman walked away.

About once an hour since landing in Korea, someone would come over and start talking to Jamie in Korean. Jamie, who had no real way of knowing what they were saying, imagined that they were asking if she had been kidnapped by the two white people who accompanied her.

A clock belltower started to play. On the ninth chime, Debussy poured from the store's loudspeakers.

"There it goes," Dad said. "Attention shoppers . . ." and they passed through the doors, which were held open by men in tuxedos.

The store clerks who had been scurrying one minute ago now stood statuesque in two lines on either side of the gold and marble corridor. Jamie led the way, gliding to "Deux Arabesques." As she passed the clerks, they fell at the waist, all in a row like dominoes in a deep bow. "*Ahn-nyong-ha-se-yo,*" they greeted her, as if she was a queen returning from a decade of valiant fighting in faraway lands. She looked at them with a mix of are-you-crazy and I-could-get-used-to-this.

After a kimchi lunch, the Amer-Asian trio went to the Holt International Post Adoption Services office where Jamie's foster family waited to see her for the first time in a dozen years. The walls in the meeting room were white and undecorated except for a calendar and a red flashlight mounted like a fire extinguisher. A Korean woman in a beige suit jacket and short haircut sat beside her college-age son at the conference table. Her son was handsome in his pink button-up shirt and red plastic frame glasses. Once he completed his two-year military service he wanted to design jewelry. A female translator was also sitting at the table, ready to help the two families communicate with each other.

As soon as Jamie walked in the room her foster mother rose reflexively. You could see the instant recognition in her eyes, even through her thick bifocals. She spoke rapidly in Korean and wrapped her arms around Jamie, smushing Jamie's budding breasts, which I'm sure Jamie would rather I not mention because she was thirteen and her body was about as comfortable to her as the silver braces in her mouth. But you need to know about those buds to understand her behavior. In her foster mom's embrace, Jamie kept a seventh-grade slow-dance distance. She was too old but too young to get any closer to the middle of her three moms in her personal motherhood chain.

Even though Jamie was not ready for the experience, as I watched the video, I realized the significance this woman had in my sister's life. I had the amazing chance to meet the women who raised Michelle, Jordan, and Meredith but not Jamie. This was as close as I could get to hers.

"She would like you to have these," the translator said as Jamie's foster mother passed Jamie and my mother duplicates of baby photos. There was Jamie on a red sofa with a plush Nintendo Mario doll bigger than she was and there she was playing a Peanuts Schroeder piano just her size. There were pictures of Jamie with nearly no hair and later pictures of her with a vertical ponytail, pointing up like a Troll doll. Her foster brother, about seven at the time, was in some photos too, ever handsome and holding her on the stone balcony outside their apartment. The final photo in the pile was of Jamie on her first birthday, her legs sitting in a W-shape and her tongue wagging at a tower of rice cakes.

"Look. I told you." Mom flashed the picture of her *tol* to Jamie.

The foster mom spoke again. "She and her son felt a special love for her, your daughter. They once thought they would like to adopt her. She has just one son."

As the translator told my parents this, the foster mom fixed the collar of her jacket. Her son, Jamie's foster brother, looked at his mom sympathetically.

"Did they foster other children after Jamie?"

"She stopped as a foster mother almost ten years ago."

"Oh, so Jamie was almost the last one."

Her foster mom patted Jamie's leg and spoke.

"She especially remembers your daughter because she took care of her so long compared to other babies."

"Yes, she was diagnosed with cerebral palsy," Mom explained. "She'd been a preemie and weighed two pounds. So it took a long time for her to be well enough to be adopted. But she took care of her. She took her to physical therapy five times a week."

The translator nodded and before she could turn the words into Hangul, Jamie's foster mother started.

"She says Jamie was a premature baby. Only weighed 1 kilogram. They had to go to physical therapy five times a week."

Jamie sipped her tea, pinky extended, to escape the awkwardness of sitting between two of her mothers telling the same story.

"She looks so healthy now," the translator said, not translating.

"Oh she is. She likes to play tennis."

"Is she now attending middle school?"

"Yes . . . very good grades. Very good student."

This made the foster mother smile, baring both rows of teeth, which were an evil dentist's dream.

"Tell her, Jamie, what you want to be when you grow up."

"A cardiothoracic surgeon."

Her foster mom's head bobbed approvingly even before the translation.

Jamie handed her foster family a present wrapped in green ribbon. It was her most recent school picture, the one with her shiny black hair touching the shoulders of a grass green shirt. "Oh!" chirped her foster mother before handing the picture frame to her son and digging in her wallet. Jamie's foster brother reached for the frame excitedly and smiled. He looked at it for a long time, examining the girl who might have been his sister, as if the real girl wasn't sitting four feet away from him.

"For you, Jamie," the translator said as the foster mom handed her a wallet-size photo of her foster brother in uniform. Jamie passed it to Mom.

"He looks so serious. He's not smiling like he does."

Mom passed it back to Jamie, who thanked her.

"Don't thank Mom. Thank her," Dad said.

Jamie turned to her foster mom who was putting her wallet away. Jamie was nervous and looked at Dad, hoping for help. Not getting any, she looked at her foster mom again. "Thank you."

"Aaah," her foster mom touched Jamie's elbow delicately like she was handling a porcelain pot. "Thank you."

"So THANK YOU FOR TRAVELING across the country, well around the world actually," Grandmother Lenore and I locked eyes, "to be here with me today." The back room at the French Café in Omaha's gentrified slaughterhouse district gargled up an off-key

"Happy Birthday" chorus. I heard someone whistle and guessed it was Michelle. After a year of being away, I had made it back to Nebraska.

The crowd mingled again and my siblings and I slinked into a corner of the brick-walled room and huddled beneath a life-size portrait of a nude woman aggressively sitting on a pile of white pillows. A second cousin came around to take our picture and we posed in a pyramid. My cheeks, neck, ribs and wrists were gaunt from circumnavigating the globe. To my right was Jordan, twenty-one, whose biceps (unlike mine) had grown in proportion to his years. Then my sisters, still stunning, posed down in front of us, smiling. They wore the beaded necklaces I had bought them from a *patua* I had met in monsoon Mumbai's jewelry district with Legs on our nose-piercing expedition.

The amateur photo shoot ended and it was just us again, all of us, for the first time in years. I pulled out the used tea box wrapped in clear packing tape Mrs. Joshi had given me in Pune.

"I know it's not your eightieth birthday but this is for you guys. From Mrs. Joshi."

"What is it?"

"No idea. I've carried it around the world and all I know is it's heavy."

Michelle used her red fingernails to cut through the layers of tape. When she got it open the smell of curry powder, pollution, and sweat escaped the box. "Yep, it's from India," she said.

Inside were three ornaments honoring BSSK's twenty-fifth birthday. They were brass and round like medals with bilingual engravings. Yellow strings were looped through the tops. Meredith suspended the ornaments on her fingers and they clattered.

Michelle looked up to me and asked, "So why did you do this anyway? Why go to India and Korea and Japan and China and Ethi-, Ethiapulous?"

"Ethiopia?"

"Yeah, why go to all those places?"

Before boarding my flight from London to Delhi and launching a twenty-three-city world tour, I wouldn't have been sure of the answer to her question. The best response I could have given would have sounded something like, "I guess I'm bored" or "I'm sick of take-out Chinese food." But there was something more that drove me to fly 24,901 miles, and I had to come full circle to know . . . to feel what I was missing. I had to find out what a little circle man's experience is. I had to hold one of the 132 million orphans in the world and then let go. I had to understand what it was to be lucky, so fucking lucky I felt nauseous thinking about it. I had to see, smell, taste, fear, and savor where my family was from and know how different life would have been for each of them if they had never become my family . . . how different *my* life would have been had they never become my family. It would have been a good life, a lucky life, if it were just me standing under the life-size portrait of a nude woman on my grandmother's birthday. But it would have been a poorer life, and I would have missed the miracles. My siblings should not have survived but they did. Four orphans from the opposite side of the planet and I should not have the same last name, but we do. I had to search the world to understand our miraculous connection that surpassed evolution, but standing beside my brother and sisters today, brought together again, it felt natural. Not normal—now I understood we weren't normal—but we felt whole for the first time in twenty years.

"Aaron? Yoo-hoo!" Michelle waved her hand in my eyes.

"Sorry . . . jetlag."

"So why'd you go all those places?"

"Let's just say I had to orbit Earth to find my way home."

"What? That's dumb. Even I know where that is on a map."

Then, without warning, I hugged her. My Ántonia. Neither of us spoke. Our embrace said everything we wanted to say. Whatever we had missed, we possessed together the precious, the incommunicable past.

THE POLICE SAID JORDAN WAS a criminal, but he would prefer to be called a "mastermind." Blogs in English, Italian, Dutch, Mandarin, Spanish, and French debated which title was more accurate. *Wired* magazine simply called him the "keypad caper" because he was the first person in U.S. history to be prosecuted for running an ATM reprogramming scam.

The morning after Grandmother Lenore's birthday party, at 11:09 AM Central Standard Time, Jordan and his sidekick entered Lobo's City Mex Restaurant in Lincoln dressed in polo shirts. It was the fourth time they had visited Lobo's that week. The manager, Raul Lobo, wasn't surprised to see them.

"These guys just had a pattern of coming into the same store right around the same time, right in order. So I just had a feeling they were going to come in today, and I said if they come into the store today, they're not leaving today."

While Lobo reached for his gun, Jordan and his cohort tinkered with the ATM. They were tricking it into giving out $20s for every $1 they withdrew. So if they asked the machine for $100, it would dispense $2,000 and they would walk out of the shop $1,900 richer. They couldn't leave Lobo's this time though. Lobo had locked the door and was pointing the gun at them.

"I did what I had to do," he said.

Jordan did, too. He tased Lobo and broke through the locked glass door to his getaway car—a 1997 Jeep Grand Cherokee that smelled like rotting cigarette ash and strawberry-kiwi Glade freshener. I had ridden in it the day before on the way home from Grandmother's party.

Lobo fired his pistol at Jordan and missed. Then he got in his car and started chasing Jordan's Jeep through the quiet streets of Lincoln. It didn't take long for the cops to notice a midday high-speed pursuit, and they eagerly joined the 70 mph caravan, like a pack of greyhounds after a rabbit.

After a few minutes the sirens and spinning lights cut Jordan's Jeep off in every direction. Jordan stopped the car, abandoned the $10,000 he'd stolen during the past week in the glove compartment, and ran through an empty building nearby. The police waited for him on the other side and cuffed him when he emerged. He was going back to the big house.

ACKNOWLEDGMENTS

A NICE BUT HONEST LADY ONCE TOLD ME it was preposterous for me to write a memoir in my twenties. She was right. That's why it is extra important for me to recognize the many people who made this book possible.

My first thanks go to Holt International, an organization that dares every day to change a child's life. They've changed mine—many times now—and for that I owe them much more than any of the royalties they will be receiving from this book. If you'd like to learn more or contribute to the work they do to find families for children around the world, visit www.HoltInternational.org.

I'm also indebted to my agent Ben Mason and editor Airié Stuart (plus her passionate team at Palgrave Macmillan) for taking this leap with me. I wouldn't have made it this far without their encouragement and better judgment.

The support of the Marshall Commission was crucial to the creation of this book.

To Stacy James, Gerry Shapiro and Julie Wheelwright, whom I've had the privilege of calling professor and friend; and to my travel companions and anyone who enabled my vagabond lifestyle by lending me a couch and a comforter (especially Neale): thank you for getting me here.

She only receives a brief mention in one story because she has already endured enough drama from my siblings and me through the years that I thought it would be kind to spare her for once, but without the loving help of our nanny Gina and her husband Andy, this book would have a very different ending.

Along those lines, I'd like to acknowledge all of the teachers who have graduated a generation of little Eske's and all of the doctors who kept us alive year after year. We didn't make your jobs easy but at least we never made them boring.

Finally, a mammoth hug for my siblings who inspired every word in this book and for Aaron who was there for me as I wrote each one. Love you. And of course to Mom and Dad who were brave/crazy enough to bring our family together twenty years ago, and then tenacious enough to keep us that way.

SOURCES OF QUOTATIONS

CHAPTER 2: FOOTSTEPS

Page 23. "Owing to this struggle for life . . .": Charles Darwin, *On the Origin of Species* (London: Murray, 1859), chapter 3.

CHAPTER 6: REINCARNATIONS

Page 92. "older than history . . .": Mark Twain, *Following the Equator: A Journey around the World* (Hartford, Conn.: American Pub. Co., 1898), 480.

CHAPTER 8: A TALE OF TWO KOREAS

Page 146. "Barring a miracle . . .": Blaine Harden, "Hunger Crisis at Heart of N. Korea's Troubles," *Washington Post,* March 6, 2009.

CHAPTER 11: HOMECOMINGS

Pages 220–221. "This was the road . . .": Willa Cather, *My Ántonia* (Boston: Houghton Mifflin, 1918), 371.

INDEX